Sex
and
Identity

Photograph by Ingbet.

Sex and Identity

B. G. Rosenberg

Bowling Green State University

Brian Sutton-Smith

Teachers College, Columbia University

HOLT, RINEHART AND WINSTON, INC.

New York   Chicago   San Francisco   Atlanta
Dallas   Montreal   Toronto   London   Sydney

To Tippy and Boysie
who gave up sex for identity.

FOREWORD

MODERN CLASSROOM TEACHERS of the psychology of personality place
a high value on diversity in selecting appropriate reading materials. They
like to choose from among "full coverage" textbooks, anthologies, journal
articles, and small books that focus on specific topics. The Person in
Psychology series was established in order to meet the need for small
textbooks that deal with important aspects of the study of persons, for
while there is an abundance of textbooks, anthologies, and journals, the
supply of small topical books is limited.

The series is devoted to in-depth reporting of relevant subjects which
are frequently included in college courses with such titles as: "Personality,"
"Socialization," "The Individual and Society," "Stress and Adaptation,"
"Personality and Culture," and "Personality and Adjustment."

In selecting topics for the series, the editor has tried to steer a middle
course between overly broad areas of study such as "Learning," "Motivation," or "Cognition," and highly specialized themes such as "Child-
Rearing Patterns in Three Island Communities" or "Bargaining Behavior
among Ghetto Youth." "Cognition," on the one hand, is too broad a topic
for a small book; on the other hand, "Bargaining Behavior among Ghetto
Youth," while timely, is too specific for most undergraduate courses. The
titles of the books published thus far indicate the not-too-broad, not-too-
narrow concept of the series. They are: *Beliefs and Values* (by Karl E.

Scheibe), *Aggression and Altruism* (by Harry Kaufmann), and *The Concept of Self* (by Kenneth A. Gergen).

The authors, besides being specialists in their respective fields, are also teachers of undergraduates, and therefore are sensitive to the needs of contemporary students. They have written from the perspective that the student is the primary reader, not the professional colleague or the professor in some distant college.

Sex and Identity is a welcome addition to the series. Professors Rosenberg and Sutton-Smith have written a fascinating account of a topic that certainly fulfills the criterion of pertinence. The relation of gender to identify-formation has too long been a forum for uninformed harangues and partially informed polemics. This book is an objective consideration of the gender components of identity, and the authors have written with an eye to the intention of providing a complete discussion.

The student who reads this book will be able to draw inferences about the multidimensioned nature of the relationship between gender and identity, for, like the authors, he will find it necessary to account for the complex data and for the diverse explanations. Nowhere else can the student obtain such a concise statement of the relevant facts on this important subject.

Theodore R. Sarbin
General Editor

University of California
Santa Cruz

ACKNOWLEDGMENTS

MANY AUTHORS, STUDENTS, AND COLLEAGUES have contributed to the syntheses presented here. We thank, to name but a few, John Paul Scott, Theodore Sarbin, Joyce Diener, Frank Beach, Donald Leventhal, Charles Keasy, Deanna Kuhn, Judith Auerbach, Jean Cryan, Aneita Sharples, Gael Goetcheus, Elmer Morgan, Marylou Teofilo, June Reinisch, Peggy Crull, Frank Landy, and most important, the principal of Kenwood School, Harland Lehtomaa. We owe a major debt to the United States Public Health Service who, for years, supported our research and writing (Grants MH 07994-01 to 08). Finally, we are particularly grateful to the host of theorists from the past from whom we as students and teachers have learned most.

B. G. Rosenberg

Brian Sutton-Smith

CONTENTS

xii   Contents

. . . All human individuals, as a result of their bi-sexual disposition and of cross-inheritance, combine in themselves both masculine and feminine characteristics, so that pure masculinity and femininity remain theoretical constructions of uncertain content [Sigmund Freud, 1925, Vol. V, p. 197].

. . . The division of the society's members into age-sex categories is perhaps the feature of greatest importance for establishing participation of the individual in culture [Linton, 1945, p. 63].

This increase in our society of conditions which favor small sex differences has led to the suggestion that we might one day virtually eliminate sex differences in socialization [Barry, Bacon, & Child, 1957, p. 331].

I

The Typological Error

THE QUOTATIONS FROM Freud, Linton, and Barry, Bacon, and Child introducing this book capture the issue to be examined: are sex differences here to stay or are they disappearing? Judging by the various theoretical approaches to be outlined in the chapters that follow, sex differences are here to stay. In most of these chapters it is assumed that being born male or female (the child's gender) has profound consequences for subsequent growth and identity. The arguments in these chapters center on whether sex role identity is determined primarily by the original biological differences between the sexes or by the subsequent differences in the way the two sexes are treated by their parents and the culture.

In this sense, the theories to be presented in this work are most conservative. In attempting to explain the development of sex and identity, the arguments assume that the future will be an extension of the past. As Mead (1969) has pointed out, in a traditional society this is a legitimate assumption. But under the contemporary circumstances, it must at least be questioned.

The rest of this introductory chapter, therefore, will wrestle with the very real problem of inevitable differences in sex and identity. By *sex* we mean the gender (male or female) with which the child is born; and by *identity* we mean the personality that is subsequently developed on the basis of that gender classification.

Perhaps the very assumption of inevitable differences between the sexes is archaic and a typological error. Individuals were once assumed to be divisible into the choleric type, the sanguine type, the phlegmatic type, and the melancholic type; or more recently, into introverts and extraverts. In effect, the view that those who are male should always be "masculine" and that those who are female should be "feminine" may be considered a

1

similar archaic typology. It is typological because the world is said to be divided into those who either one type or the other. It may be considered an error because psychologists generally do not find such simple classifications a valid way of handling differences in human personality, though in common parlance sex role stereotypes about masculinity and femininity are both pervasive and persistent. Men who prefer knitting are labeled "feminine" if not worse, and women who enjoy forensics are labeled "masculine" and usually worse. In fact, women and men vary among themselves as well as between themselves, and what comes out of any empirical study are complex, multidimensional individual differences as well as the reports on those gross and simple differences between the average scores of the two groups on which this typology is based. That is, males or females often differ as much or more from one another as they do from the opposite sex.

Furthermore, the behavior that is given the same *name* for both sexes is usually not the same in character, origin, or development. This makes even the typological comparisons spurious in nature. Thus, if nurturance is found significantly more often in females, then the observation of this behavior in a male may be taken to mean that he is possessed of greater femininity than the average male. It is far more likely, however, that if a man and woman are seen as "equally nurturant," the paths to this status have been remarkably dissimilar, with a very different relevance for the total personality. For example, Helson (1968) investigated the personality elements in highly creative mathematicians and architects. She found that ". . . creative men, in comparison with other men, showed a combination of enrichment of personality, intellectual assertiveness, and outer direction," whereas, ". . . creative women, in comparison with other women, showed a pattern of receptivity to emotional stimuli, intellectual direction and control, 'brooding,' need for autonomous self-expression, and resistance to outer expression of femininity [p. 44]." These members of each sex encountered different gender-related problems and, in their particular adaptations to these problems, arrived at a degree of apparently similar behavior as highly creative architects and mathematicians.

Again, what is often viewed as a gender-specific response may sometimes be more appropriately viewed as unrelated to sex role identity. Thus, though nurturant behavior is viewed as more typical of females in our culture, such behavior in a father-son or father-daughter interaction may be unrelated to the nature of the father's sex role and unrelated to his sex-typed activity. It may on occasion be more appropriate to assign it to his personal rather than his sexual identity.

When it comes to the measurement of masculine-feminine differences, the problems which arise are of a similar order to those just mentioned: namely, the neglect of differences within each sex, the naming of things as the same which are really different, and the assigning to sex role of attributes which are personal or human rather than specifically sexual in nature. For example, scores of studies using the Gough Femininity Scale (1952) ask questions such as the following, to which females most often respond as indicated:

"I like to boast about my achievements every now and then." (False)

"I am inclined to take things hard." (True)

"Sometimes I have this same dream over and over." (True)

"I like to go to parties and other affairs where there is lots of loud fun." (False)

In this scale, as in many others, gross differences between the sexes, sampled in such a limited fashion, are then used for attributing high or low femininity scores to particular subjects. Characteristically, the male with a high femininity score is expected to be generally feminine in nature, and the investigator usually finds some correlations with other female characteristics which are taken to support this assumption. Yet, as we have just explained, even in these gross terms, the scores made by males may have a meaning quite different from those same scores made by females. The term "feminine" girl has a connotation different from the term "feminine" man. Their scores on this test may be similar, but most of their behavior is not.

More important, to use such simple dipstick measures is to assume that sex role is a unified entity that can be legitimately sampled in any one phase. But if sex role characteristics are like personality characteristics, then they are most likely to be multifaceted. Thus behavior of one order (courting) may be quite unlike behavior of another order (gaming), and behavior within one order (courting), may vary considerably across situations (in the parlor vs. in the back seat of an auto). Which is to say, again, that any single test is likely to give us a most unrepresentative sample of a subject's "masculinity" or "femininity."

Whatever psychological masculinity-femininity is, therefore, it represents extremely diverse phenomena, best viewed as a loose cluster of imprecisely defined behavioral correlates. With the exception of the assessment device provided by Terman and Miles (1936), few if any current instruments attempt to measure these many different aspects of the sex role. A possible solution to this problem remains available but, thus far, relatively uninvestigated. There exists a large and rich literature on sex differences in all motor, perceptual, and motivational realms, often obtained as a by-product of experimental investigation (Garai & Schein-feld, 1968). It is probable that the structural differences described by this literature, if used in a "multiphasic-like" assessment, could provide the basis for a test of far greater validity than most present assessments. Another relatively unexplored pathway in psychological research is the extensive analysis of individual differences within each sex, which could provide parameters for typical behavior within as well as between the sexes.

If we ask why the present psychometric oversimplifications persist, the answers are not easy to discover. It sometimes seems as if common sense and empirical data cannot coincide because here, as in politics, the extremes are polarized and feed defensively upon each other. The single-minded man of adventure and the hearth-bound woman require each other's existence to justify their own asymmetry. These may be men and women who both feel threatened by any suggestion that either should depart from the traditional form of personality organization; or more simply, they may be men and women who feel it is stupid to depart from so comfortable an arrangement. Or perhaps, as some radical feminists contend, the present typology promotes the interests of men, who, by thus obscuring the possibilities for individual personality development, can continue to keep women in a largely subservient role. If *female* progress can be scorned, as contended by the feminists, then individual differences co-occurring with femaleness can be minimized, and more than half the population can be confined to menial occupations. It is, of course, unlikely that most men are intelligent enough to be consciously machiavellian in arranging such a system, but it is not unlikely that traditional differences whose origins are obscured would be rationalized by those who would gain from their continuation. It is much easier for a man to argue that childcare as well as childbirth is more natural to women if this alleviates his responsibility for getting out of bed in the middle of the night to feed the baby. Here, what appears as common sense or intuitive insight is prompted by a very large measure of hidden personal comfort.

To the psychologist then, the persistence of the typology is something of a puzzle, not only because it makes limited psychometric sense, but also because most forms of status (class, race, caste, or primogeniture) seem to be declining in importance. He might argue that sex as a form of status seems also to be disappearing and that individual differences in personality are taking its place as terms of reference for human characteristics. As a reflection of this change, he might further argue that recent evidence has revealed discontinuities in cultural values, socializing agents, and role requirements for sex differences, so that preparing children for varying and ambiguous cultural requirements has resulted in decreasing clarity in sex role prescription and sex role training. The past several decades have seen a decreasing level of consensus on sex role behaviors in American society. With men and women sharing a realm of behaviors that were formerly assigned to one sex or the other, the impossibility of careful delineation in adult sex roles has led to difficulties in identifying what early social experiences an individual *should* encounter in order to best prepare him for appropriate role adoption. One can be convinced of this when examining the small difference in the socialization of boys and girls manifest in our society at the present time. This increase in conditions that favor fewer sex differences has led to the suggestion that we might one day virtually eliminate sex differences in socialization. Even now, fewer sex differences is a characteristic of the socioeconomically and educationally advantaged segments of Western society.

An anthropologist might retort, however, that any apparent decrease in differences between the sexes (and therefore, decrease in usefulness of the typology) is a relatively superficial phenomenon and has been restricted to certain socioeconomic groups in the recent history of Western culture. No matter what disservice the typology might appear to do to individual differences, he would argue, it has always been a mainstay of human societies everywhere. To reiterate Linton: (1945) "The division of the society's members into age-sex categories is perhaps the feature of greatest importance for establishing participation of the individual in culture [p. 63]."

To an anthropologist, therefore, there may be no typological error at all. The typology is a universal cultural reality, and finding "psychological" reasons for its persistence in the form of male dominance or male defensiveness is uneconomical in that it involves using particular and local explanations when more universal explanations are at hand. The anthropologist would also explain why psychologists, paradoxically, persist in using this typology: as members of a culture, they are deeply affected by the same dual sex role value system the anthropologist observes to be so prevalent throughout history and society. This involvement permits the psychologists to persist in using a measurement device in the area of sex differences that they would disregard in the realm of personality experimentation.

This, then, is the statement of the problem: on the one hand is increasing contemporary evidence of diminishing differences in identity between males and females, but on the other hand is the larger context of history and anthropology, which suggests that in our "modernism" we may protest too much, that there is still good reason for continued use of this classification of masculine and feminine types.

Having thus stated though not resolved the typology (we will return to the matter in the final chapter), we move next to a consideration of various theories regarding the development of sex and identity. Although all these theories begin with the assumption that sex differences are a continuing reality, their arguments on behalf of that reality may contribute a decision as to its future. Is the anthropological evidence as binding as implied above? What of the biological evidence? Is it equally binding?

We forewarn the reader that apparent simplifications in the treatment of this masculine-feminine typology are unfortunately paralleled by simplicities in the theoretical approaches. In the past several decades, much effort has been devoted to the development of unicausal systems to explain sex role development. If femininity and masculinity are indeed singular entities, then they might possibly have singular explanations like those that are to be found in psychoanalytic or social learning theory. In part, of course, this singularity is not specific to sex role interpretation but is characteristic of social science in general. Theories in social science tend to be miniature theories only, sometimes useful for conceptualizing certain types of data in certain types of contexts and for making predictions within those limits, but not often useful in more general ways, although wider claims are usually made. Paradoxically, the making of such exaggerated claims may harness the "missionary-like" enthusiasm of young inquirers who, in turn, push the theory so far that they reveal its conceptual and empirical limits.

Whatever the reason for these oversimplifications, however, whether they lie in the typological error or in propagandistic theoretical enthusiasms, any approach to the subject of sex and identity must confront a number of alternative explanations. It can be assumed that one of the theories is correct, or that they are all wrong, or that they are all partially correct. If it is true that sex role identity is, like personality, multifaceted, then it is most likely that they are all partially correct. If that is the case, it might be possible to look at each theory in turn to see what particular truth it has to offer about sex and identity. Putting together the limited perspectives extending across the theories, it should be possible to gain some useful notions about the entire question. That is the intention of this book. Let it be said by way of skeptical advance, however, that each theory spins such a verbal system that it is sometimes hard to know what makes sense and what makes magic. It is not easy to know whether the language of each system uniquely captures the reality it construes, so that each language system touches a different part of the proverbial elephant, and thus by examining each language we can reveal the whole elephant. In contrast, there may be no elephant at all, merely the need for quite different languages. Still, the way to resolve this issue is to review the existing languages.

Each of the theories is described in its own terms and allowed to speak for itself to its critics. In succeeding chapters the contributions of comparative psychology, physiological psychology, psychoanalysis, social learning, sociology, and anthropology are examined. The emphasis in this work is on theoretical approaches. By beginning with comparative and animal data, we might appear to favor the reductionist prejudice that sex and identity are predominantly under hereditary control. And by ending with anthropology, we might equally appear to favor the view that all is determined by the larger cultural context. Instead, we see ourselves as proceeding from a language that deals with one type of gross limit over behavior to another language that deals with a different type of gross limit. Biology and anthropology discuss the outer limits of what is *given* in the simplest sense, while the intervening chapters on psychoanalysis, social learning, and sociology discuss what is *taken* and how it is taken by the functioning individual. Sex role identity is for the present authors a transactional question involving the gross controls of the media (heredity and culture) and the fine controls of the unit (the psychosexual individual) functioning within the limits of those media. But we will have more to say about these matters in a concluding chapter, after we have gleaned what is to be gained from these unique languages.

II

The Language of the Comparative Psychologist

T HERE ARE SEVERAL REASONS for studying sex role behavior among animals. Originally, such study was based on a belief, derived from biology, that because there was continuity across species, then much was to be learned by the study of resemblances between man and other forms of life. It was said, in agreement with Darwin, that the structure and function of each species could be understood only by knowledge of the structure and function of animals lower in the hierarchy of development. This view was sustained by a genetic bias in social science, which asserted that the study of origins provides an explanation for behavior. However, we now know that all this method of study can do is provide information about origins. The simplistic bias, which contends that because animal life is less complex it will provide prototypic explanations for the complex behavior of human beings, is a rather old-fashioned view, one no longer held by scientists. In essence, it implies that the "lower animals" are "on the way" to becoming human, when they are actually on the way to becoming something else, different in each case. Despite the more recent standpoints regarding both of these biases, they are currently being manifested in a rash of books with such titles as *The Territorial Imperative, The Naked Ape, Crazy Ape,* and so on, which suggest that the purported simplicities of animal existence provide some key to man's current and increasingly complex cultural confusions.

All that these exercises really demonstrate is that the animal scene is itself sufficiently complex to be used to support the interpretive foci that scholars bring to it about human beings. This is not to say that such usage must be regarded as completely inadmissible. It is reasonable to examine

9

the universality of hominid-focused theories employing the comparative materials. It is reasonable also that novel information from animal studies should be used at least to provoke new questions about human behavior. But perhaps most important of all in scientific work, animals are suitable for the controlled observations and environmental manipulation as well as the surgical and hormonal intervention that is generally impossible with human subjects. Only accidents yield predictable variants of normal human sexual behavior. More often, knowledge about human sexual behavior is obtained from subjective reports (with the major exception being the work of Masters & Johnson, 1965, 1968), while animal sexual behavior is obtained from reliable observation and measurement of discrete components of behavior (Whalen, 1966). Again, human sexual motivation is discussed in terms of hypothetical constructs (e.g., libido), while animal sexual behavior is discussed in response terms (e.g., frequency, latency). Cyclic variations of sexual activity and seasonal variations in animals, absent in humans, allow for semicontrolled observation. The advantages that these approaches make use of include the shorter life span, the availability of subsequent generations for study, and the ease with which sexual behavior can be manipulated in captive lower animals as contrasted with man.

On the other hand, it is important to note that the greater portion of the evidence on animal sexual behavior comes from laboratory animals removed from their natural habitat, those within their own surroundings being more difficult to observe. We are saying that what we know about animal sexual behavior comes from more controlled quantifiable situations than the natural setting; but at the same time, it is usually studied using a less representative methodology than would be desired, and may involve behaviors that vary in form and sequence when the animal is removed from its natural setting. Still, the point is that when comparing the methodologies with those employed on humans, these techniques show merit.

In sum, the following reasons are the major justifications for employing the comparative method of study: (1) it may result in general laws applying to all living beings including man; (2) it may give rise to ideas that may or may not apply to man but that can be confirmed by experimental testing; and (3) animals may serve as experimental models for human problems. This last procedure, incidentally, is by far the most difficult and most subject to error.

On one hand, the danger in using animal data to interpret human data is that we may see parallels where none, in fact, exist. On the other hand, some theories hold that each species evolves independently, and it is simply not possible to recreate the history of mankind by looking at other species (Scott, 1970). If we ignore the data from animal behavior, we run the risk of seeing as uniquely human certain phenomena that are found in all species. Either way, we hazard interpretive distortions. On these grounds it seems wise to begin with a general account of the information on animals in order to establish the outer biological limits within which interpretations are to be confined.

No doubt there is much to be learned from the study of animal behavior. What really prompts us to review some of the research and theory here is the desire to understand the primacy of biological and experiential determinants of sex role behavior, which may be more readily revealed in animals. After all, ignoring for the moment whatever implications there may be for man, the study of animal behavior provides a paradigm involving a range from primitive to highly complex structures, functions, and behaviors that are obtainable nowhere else. In addition, it affords a high degree of precision when one is seeking to determine the influence of chromosomal and hormonal factors on sex role behavior. Thus, the problems we face have to do with the relative importance of sexual differentiation in phylogenesis, and with the relative importance of genetic, hormonal, and experiential determinants in sexual behavior.

SEXUAL BEHAVIOR IN ANIMALS

The range of sexual behavior in animals is remarkably varied and elaborate. It extends from the asexual behavior in the coelenterate (a marine animal) to the complex mating behaviors of higher primates akin to man. Although the primary function of sexual behavior is fertilization, as we ascend the phylogenetic scale sexual behavior becomes closely related to the development and proliferation of social groupings. In the invertebrates sex activity may be as simple as cell division in paramecia, while in mammals it may be as complicated as the conjugated seasons, mating behaviors, courtships, and copulatory activities of the elephant seal. The evidence appears to indicate that animals who have the capacity for sexual reproduction evolve more rapidly than those who do not, for sexual reproduction provides a population with tremendous genetic variability unobtainable in asexual reproduction. Such variability usually aids in the continuing survival of at least some members of the population under conditions that are lethal to most of that group of organisms (Freedman, 1968).

The sexual behavior of animals other than man appears to be regulated more by genetic and structural factors than by acquired preferences.

Unlike man, the animal's system of reproduction is ordered by the presence of estrous cycles in the female which are governed by hormonal actions, and by the consequent seasonal variations in receptivity. As we ascend the scale of phylogeny, the general evolutionary tendency is toward greater differentiation of sexual behavior, males becoming more active and dominant, females becoming more passive. Scott (1961) has suggested that this is associated with production of eggs by the female, which tend to be heavy and bulky. In addition, animals that are relatively mobile appear to have evolved sexual behavior in order to reproduce in a more efficient way, whereas more sluggish animals can rely on less elaborate sexual behaviors or, as in the case of some, asexual reproduction.

It seems clear that as we go from simpler to more complex animals, sexual activity becomes less solely related to fertilization and increasingly related to social behavior. In some species, it is true, sexual behavior does not have a role in the social life of the animal (e.g., herd animals), while in others it appears to be central to the development of social behavior (e.g., wolves). For reasons not fully understood, as we move from less to more complex animals there is a tendency for instinctive behaviors to become more variable and diffuse, and consequently, for individual experience to play a more subtle and intricate role in forming those responses into biologically effective patterns (Mason, 1965). It may be that lengthening the period of postnatal dependency tends to increase the opportunity and necessity for the more intense, elaborate, and enduring social relationships found in these higher mammals and man. However, even with the instinctive sexual striving in lower animals it is often difficult to determine the precise causal agent when seeking to establish a link between sexual motivation and social behavior. For some animals, such as the elk or moose, the estrous period is very brief, no other sexual behaviors occur, and the males and females show little other relationship to one another. In the case of wolves, on the other hand, mated pairs frequently live together throughout the year and exhibit courtship patterns. This so-called extended sexual behavior, found in some of the primates and characteristic of man, "extends the function of sexual behavior far beyond that of fertilization [Scott, 1961, p. 140]." Generally speaking then, while the sexual and social behaviors of some animals are highly similar to those of man, there are other animals similar in level of development and complexity which show behaviors totally unlike those of man. While there is some evidence that sex-related behaviors (e.g., dominance, aggression) do obtain phylogenetically, a cursory examination suggests that phylogenetic parameters of sex role behavior are less common than might be expected.

GENETIC AND HORMONAL DETERMINANTS

The point has been presented that animal sex role behavior is predetermined genetically to a greater extent than that of man. Though a large segment of the research literature attests to this idea, it is perhaps too readily assumed that lower animals are motivated only by instinct. In fact, we are only now beginning to understand the elements of inheritance and their interaction with hormonal factors. In insects, for example, chromosomal factors generally seem to be the primary determinants of sex, secondary sexual characteristics, and sexual behavior, while hormonal influences are apparently negligible. But there are some instances in which mating behavior even in insects does not appear to be independent of hormonal organizing effects. It may be enlightening to pursue at least one example with insects, to depict the intricacies in the relationship of genes and hormones to sexual behavior.

In many insects, mating behavior appears to be independent of control by hormones (Caspari, 1965), although in certain species, it has been shown to be influenced by the secretion of endocrine glands, the corpora allata, which are small glands situated close to the brain. It has been known for a long time that the corpora allata secrete a hormone during larval development which, in collaboration with the hormone of a second gland (prothoracic gland), is responsible for larval molts. During the last larval instar, the corpora allata do not produce their hormone, and the resulting molt, induced by the prothoracic glands alone, leads to a pupa. In the late pupa and in the adult, the corpora allata resume their hormonal activity. Thus, extirpation experiments with roaches and grasshoppers revealed that diminished mating behaviors do, in fact, occur. This finding cannot be generalized, however, for similar removal does not always inhibit mating behaviors in these same groups of insects. Thus, on occasion, in the same order of insects hormonal control as well as independence from hormones may be found. Caspari (1965) hypothesizes that hormonal control of sexual behavior is a secondary function, arguing that the genes determine whether gonads will develop in a male or female direction. Other sexual characteristics (e.g., morphological and behavioral) are subsequently controlled by sex hormones secreted by the gonads and distributed by the bloodstream. Caspari suggests that gene determination is the prime element even in late mating behavior. In contrast, Chang and Witschi (1956) argue that genes play an active role only during a limited period, and subsequent to this time hormones are the effective agents. This latter viewpoint serves as an example of the disagreements marring generalizations about exclusive genetic controls—even with insects.

When we move to higher levels, the evidence does appear to indicate that gonadal hormones increasingly organize patterns of behavior. Phoenix, Goy, Gerall, and Young (1959) demonstrated that female guinea pigs are behaviorally as well as somatically masculinized by an androgen (testosterone propionate) prenatally injected into the mother; the female offspring, for example, exhibited male-like mounting behavior. The same results were obtained with rhesus monkeys. That prenatally administered androgens will masculinize the normal female behavior patterns and genital structures was confirmed by research done by Young, Goy, and Phoenix (1964). In species that show only seasonal breeding, the males as well as the females are inactive hormonally as well as behaviorally except for the particular period of the breeding season. Castration of certain animals (e.g., rabbits, guinea pigs, hamsters, and mice), which reduces the concentration of testosterone (some continues to be produced by the adrenal glands), is followed by a rapid decline of sexual behavior. As Beach (1958) notes: "It is clear that in these animals the susceptibility to sexual arousal and the capacity to mate are heavily dependent upon secretory activity of the reproductive glands [pp. 274–275]."

Another approach to the influence of hormones is through the study of sex differences across species. Beach (1958, p. 271) notes that in females of most lower mammalian species, sexual behavior is heavily dependent upon hormones secreted by the ovaries. Sexual behavior in these species is typically exhibited only when the related hormones are present in sufficient concentrations. Mating responses are lacking in prepubertal animals, and the first display of receptive behavior coincides with the second or third full estrous cycle, the first ones often being "silent heat." Prepubertal females treated with ovarian hormones tend to exhibit behavior similar to that of more mature females, further confirming the significant role of hormones in sex role activity. A characteristic of most animals is that when a female is not physiologically in estrus, she is not exciting to the male and will not permit coitus (Beach, 1958, p. 272). In these species removal of the ovaries results in prompt and permanent loss of the female's sexual receptivity. Other hormonal secretions directly influence sexual responsiveness in the higher primates, especially when the animal's estrogen level is high. However, unlike the infraprimates, these females will permit occasional sexual activity during the periods when the ovaries are relatively quiescent.

For the male primate the story is somewhat different. While female animals lower than the primate (e.g., rodents and carnivores) never exhibit adult mating patterns prior to estrus, young males frequently exhibit aspects of the adult male response well before the onset of puberty:

pursuing, clasping, and mounting (albeit ineffectively). The absence of any amount of the sex hormone (androgen) in these young males suggests that these are learned activities (Harlow, 1962). If the prepubertal male is treated with androgens, he then exhibits true adult sexual behavior. That is, he will assume the complete sex posture which involves ankle clasping, dorsoventral mounting, and clasping of the female's buttocks.

Thus, many gender-specific (e.g., physical features) and sex-related (e.g., aggressive behavior) phenomena in infrahuman primates are extensively influenced by the prenatal and postnatal presence or absence of gonadal hormones, though there are some sexually differentiated behaviors apparently uninfluenced by hormones.

According to Young (1965), who summarized a series of studies bearing on the relationship of hormones to sexual appearance and behavior in rats and monkeys, the prenatal or early postnatal period is the time when gonadal hormones have an *organizing action* on the tissues that will mediate mating behavior in the adult. In these studies, females injected with testosterone showed a remarkable change in sexual behavior, for example, a decrease in estrus cycles, a shorter duration of heat, more male-like mountings, and so on. In the case of an older animal, a temporary masculinization of genital structure and sexual behavior occurred, with early remission of this behavior. The pregnant adult female appeared to be refractory to such effects, though the foetus was not. In these studies, it seemed that testosterone propionate affected the developing central nervous system, resulting in the production of the male phenotype. The implications are that much of sexual behavior in animals is directly related to gene determination and the timing of hormonal release.

Still, it should be kept in mind that the importance of hormonal factors in sexual motivation has been demonstrated primarily with birds, rodents, and other lower animals (Beach, 1958). In this light, care must be exerted in generalizing to more complex animals, for example, higher primates. Though hormonal influences on sexual behavior are strong, there is no simple one-to-one antecedent-consequent relationship, even here. In some species of mice, for example, males responded to injections of male hormones with increased aggressiveness, while females responded to these hormones, not reflecting a masculinizing effect, but with an *increase* in appropriate sexual behavior. Such evidence suggests that there are, in fact, central nervous system differences in males and females.

In summary, the suggestion has been advanced that genes are crucial in sex role behavior in that they exert a complex influence on the developing central nervous system. One might construe this to be placing the emphasis on brain chemistry and structure, that is, genes predispose to certain brain structures which subsequently act as a potentiated medium for later hormonal influences. In this view then, hormones consequently play a secondary, albeit crucial role. On the other hand, a number of studies reinforce the usefulness of a hormonal-sexual behavior relationship, as we have seen. The evidence to clarify this precedence in the relationship to ultimate behavior is not available at this time. The latter position is somewhat weakened by the paradox that adult sex-appropriate behavior can be initiated by the injection of hormones, while at the same time, some sex-appropriate behaviors are present in absence of hormones. In addition, the most convincing hormone-behavior relationships tend to obtain with animals below the primate level (e.g., birds, rodents), but even in these lower animals one must exert caution in pinpointing a causal basis for sex role behavior.

We must be careful in generalizing these causal factors to higher animals as well as to man in view of the frequent demonstration of the diminishing influence of genetic and hormonal determinants on sexual behavior, and the increasing prominence of experience and learning in these higher species (Beach, 1947; Ford & Beach, 1951; Harlow, 1962). In the case of human sex role behavior genetic-hormonal interpretations certainly prove less than adequate in accounting for the complexity noted. The point to be made in briefly assaying the literature on chromosomes and hormones as determinants of sexual behavior in lower animals is that there are alternate ways in which chromosomal sexual constitution may affect mating behavior: either directly, by controlling the genetic constitution of the brain cells, or indirectly, by initially determining the sex organs and hormones secreted by them, with the reaction of the brain thus dependent upon the quality of the hormonal stimulus (Caspari, 1965, p. 45).

HORMONAL AND EXPERIENTIAL DETERMINANTS

If we shift our focus from the genetic-hormonal relations to hormonal-experiential relations, we find that phenomena in both are equally complex. As shown above, animal sex role behavior is not understandable on the basis of presence and amount of hormones alone. When castrated animals were injected with the same amount of testosterone propionate, they displayed the types of behavior which had characterized their performance before castration; that is individual differences persisted when the animals contained equal levels of testosterone in their systems (Grunt & Young, 1952). These continuing individual differences cannot be accounted for solely on the basis of the *levels* of gonadal hormones, but appear to be determined by the quality of the tissues on which the hormones must act (Young, 1965, p. 89). Thus, it is not at all unlikely that animals generally respond to hormonal presence with behaviors which are similar. At the same time, a residue of potentiated neural tissue and past experience account for the variety of sexual behaviors that are possible for the animal. In a sense then, we are saying that hormonal activation occurs in the context of the overall disposition to behave which is conditioned by the animal's unique neural structures and his past experience with such behaviors.

In addition, the timing of the masculinizing effect of exogenous testosterone propionate suggests that there are fairly specific prenatal and early postnatal periods during which it is possible to alter the neurologic apparatus of the organism and consequently produce nontypical behavior (Young, 1965, pp. 91–93). Young concludes that "when the developing female guinea pig is subjected to the influence of androgen, the neural tissues mediating mating behavior are affected in such a way that there is a suppression of the capacity to display the feminine components [p. 95]." In addition, he states, "What is implied, therefore, is that in the central nervous system, as in the genital system of the embryonic female guinea pig, there are substrates which react differentially depending on whether testes or ovaries are present [pp. 95–96]."

The hormonal basis of reproductive cycles in baboons and its influence on the male sex role has been clearly depicted in a report by DeVore (1965). Studying monkeys in a free-ranging group in their natural setting, DeVore describes the importance of *dominance hierarchies* in baboons. These dominance hierarchies constitute the most stable series of dominance relationships in the troop, and include only fully adult males. Hormonally initiated cycles of sexual receptivity in females evoke copulatory activity on the part of the dominant male. His particular position or role in the dominance hierarchy is directly related to his opportunities to copulate with fully estrous females. The dominant male forms a consort with the fully tumescent female lasting from a few hours to a few days, the duration depending on how many other females are available and how much the pair is harassed by other males. The female is attractive to the dominant adult male only during the period of maximum tumescence, but during partial swelling the lesser males (juveniles, subadults, and less dominant adult males) may exhibit sexual activity because of the lack of competition. What we have described appears to be a direct relationship between hormonal activity and tumescence in the females, and social ordering and sexual activity in the male baboons. It is worth noting that such relationships are not always that straightforward, and situational stimuli may, in fact, alter the hormonal activity and subsequent behavior. Thus, DeVore (1965, p. 286) notes that even when a female baboon is in full tumescence, the occurrence of a sudden fight or attack causes rapid detumescence which may last for several hours.

Aronson (1965) presents an interesting summary of how light and temperature influence sexual stimulation. The indirect influence involves one or more sensory systems bringing stimuli to higher nerve centers, which in turn initiate glandular activities and gonad-stimulating hormones (Aronson, 1965, p. 291). For example, increasing temperature induces gonadal maturation in a variety of fishes. This is correlated with aggressive courtship and breeding behavior. In the case of sticklebacks, for example, a sudden rise in temperature is a powerful stimulus to spawning behavior.

In sum, despite the occasional contradictions that occur and the varied methodologies employed, it seems reasonable to conclude that gonadal hormones organize certain patterns of behavior in lower vertebrates as well as in mammals. As we reported in the previous section, some investigators (e.g., Chang & Witschi, 1956) have argued that the importance of gonadal hormones may even transcend that of the genes. The most precise conclusion regarding all lower species which we can draw at this point is that the genes play an active role for a short period of time, and thereafter, hormones and experience become the effective agents.

SEX AND SEX RELATED ROLE

This section will present the nonreproductive structures and activities which are sexually dimorphic or "gender-related." Male and female sexual activity in humans may be better understood by a preliminary consideration of these sex-related behaviors found in higher animals as well as in man.

Most prominent among these dimorphisms are differences in size and strength, an extreme example being seals and related marine carnivores. Male elephant seals are as much as two and one-half, and male fur seals ten times the size of their females. Although this is extreme, a difference of approximately fifty percent is not at all rare among mammals, with the male tending to be bigger and heavier than the female (Freedman, 1968, p. 267) in the majority of mammals. In light of this, it is in no way surprising to find gender-specific behavior in males including forms of aggression and dominance. Horns and antlers, as in many species of deer, are in many instances differentiated between sexes. Teeth which can function effectively as weapons are also frequent secondary sex characteristics of mammalian males, such as the enlarged canine teeth of male baboons, and, an extreme example, the single large tooth of the male narwhal. The spurs of the rooster represent an example of male-female structural variations related to role differences in birds.

What this means is that most species demonstrate male-female appurtenances which are not directly sexual but can be most appropriately considered sex-related. It may be, as expressed by Harlow (1965), that the appearance of the preadolescent heterosexual stage is first expressed in gender-specific response patterns not directly related to actual heterosexual behavior. For example, threatening behavior is considered a basic social activity characteristic of rhesus monkeys. In the first nine months it is relatively frequent in both male and female monkeys, though after two or three months males show greater evidence of this behavior, with females exhibiting a decrease in frequency. In addition, males increase in directing threat responses toward both males and females, while females begin to direct this response only toward females. The characteristic female sexual reaction is withdrawal at the time of interaction, especially with threatening male monkeys. Harlow notes that these patterns of behavior probably do not originate in learning since these activities are found even in animals with mechanical, inanimate surrogate mothers. Withdrawal and passivity decline in overall frequency in both sexes, but occur more often in females. Males withdraw from other males on occasion, but never from females, and, as we noted above, most female withdrawal responses are initiated by male activity. It is noteworthy that this same sex difference holds for the postural pattern of passivity in copulatory activity. As for the play activity engaged in by infant monkeys, it is typically rough and tumble, and as might be predicted, the male is the initiator. At the later stage males continue to engage in contact play, whereas this activity decreases in females (quite analogous to play characterizing young humans). Harlow concludes "that basic response patterns which are not directly heterosexual may nevertheless insure that normal heterosexual posturing will be acquired as long as normal infant-infant affectional responses are given an adequate opportunity to develop [p. 243]." Thus, it appears that if the young animal is exposed to a normative environment, integration of these behaviors into appropriate sexual patterns does occur.

In an additional note regarding sex-related behavior, Harlow observes that "grooming" behavior becomes a predominantly female preoccupation after five or six months, with little possibility that it is learned from the mother as she appears to behave in respect to grooming without concern for the sex of the young. In the absence of a real mother and an opportunity for learning such sex-appropriate responses, Harlow concludes, "It is extremely difficult for us to believe that these differences are cultural, for we cannot imagine how our inanimate surrogate mothers could transmit culture to their infants [p. 240]." Harlow's findings indicate that the appearance of gender-related behaviors (e.g., passivity, withdrawal, rigidity, play roles, and grooming) occurs even in the absence of an opportunity for learning. One may conclude from his research that many sex role differences in infants are biologically determined, though a final decision would require more precise observations. According to Harlow, then, normal mating behavior will occur if normal affectional responses develop, demonstrating that other factors besides gonadal sufficiency are necessary for copulatory activity in animals.

The interrelationships of structural factors (morphology) and experience are further seen in the baboons mentioned earlier. In the case of the baboon, as we have already seen, DeVore (1965) indicates that adult male dominance hierarchies constitute the most stable and rigidly maintained series of relationships in the troop. The hierarchy may contain a single adult male who is dominant and controls the group, or it may contain two or three adult males working in cooperation to maintain the dominant role in the group. DeVore studied the baboon in its natural habitat, and his observations differ somewhat from the literature on the sexual behavior of captive animals, indicating that captivity may seriously disturb the social relationships and the mating behaviors of these animals. According to DeVore, the more dominant the adult male, the greater his opportunities to copulate. Intriguingly, DeVore notes, "A male's dominance status, as revealed by his access to incentives such as estrous females, depends not so much on his status as an individual as upon his participation in a mutually supportive group of males—the central hierarchy [p. 283]."

Again, although the sexually dimorphic behaviors occur independent of normal sexual behavior in animals, it is likely that they serve some preadaptive function for adult heterosexual behavior. Young female baboons play less than young males and spend a portion of their time grooming adult females, especially if these adult females have black infants younger than six months of age. The juvenile female is evidently very attracted to these infants and attempts to handle them frequently. It is possible to construe this behavior as preadaptive mothering responses in the juveniles. In regard to the higher primates it is reasonable to speculate that sexual behavior which characterizes normal adults is contingent less on maturation and physiological functioning than it is on the "formation of tendencies or capacities for a general social responsiveness out of which more specific types of interindividual reaction patterns can later emerge [Beach, 1965, p. 549]." DeVore (1965) adds, "The full range of adult masculine behavior patterns cannot ordinarily be given expression until the male has won his way to the upper levels of the male hierarchy. It is probable that this does not usually occur until the tenth or eleventh year of life (despite his potency at five years of age) [p. 268]." Normal mating behavior will occur only if the male has a high place in the troop hierarchy.

Briefly, we are saying that while the genetic and hormonal variables are unquestionably influential, sex-related behaviors and experiences are necessary for normal adult sex role behavior in the higher animals.

Looking back over the contents of this chapter, we see that the comparative approach emphasizes the evolutionary character of sex role behavior, focusing upon the characteristics that obtain across species despite changes in structure and function. This approach tends to heighten similarities rather than differences. Heredity (via chromosomes and hormones) is seen as the organizing influence in sexual behavior in invertebrates and vertebrates, and thus may be judged relevant to sex role behavior in humans. Emphasis is placed on the role of reflex activity, with hormonal variables as primary determinants, although as we have seen, there are increasingly complex interrelationships between genetic, hormonal, and experiential influences as we move up the scale of animal development. Some of the interrelationships are quite complicated and not well understood at this point. But it is clear that no simplistic account of causal bases and behavioral outcomes is sufficient by itself. Where we have emphasized the extent to which genetic and hormonal factors account for the greater portion of the variance in complex sex role behavior in animals lower than man, the question still remains regarding the nature of their interaction, the neural mediators, and the significant (if lesser) role played by experience.

Attempts to apply these findings to human sexual behavior are fraught with difficulty. Though hormonal variables are important determinants of sex role behavior in animals, they are clearly of diminished relevance in the understanding of such behavior in humans. The seasonal variations in animal sexual behavior find little counterpart in that of the human. While note can be made of the relationship of sex and size to behavioral correlates in animals, sex role behavior in humans appears to take on a function secondary to that of social coherence and coordination, that is, to the development of social roles. Furthermore, the closer we look at the sexual activity of nonhuman species, the more this resembles that of humans, rather than vice versa. While it would indeed be satisfying to ignore the possible plasticity in animal behavior and suggest that exceptions to genetic hormonal control are infrequent enough not to be of concern, noncritical generalizations about animals are as ensnaring a conceptual "box" as that which binds the environmentalist to the statement that *all* behavior is learned. In the course of emphasizing gender-specific characteristics, it is important to make note of the apparent contradictions that *do* exist, suggesting certain limits, stressed in the previous survey, on the overriding influence of genetic-hormonal predispositions. There are strong individual differences within as well as between species. Ginsburg (1965) points out that fights among the female wolves he has studied are far more severe than fights among the males, though this is generally not the case with animals. The dominant male appears to rule by threats and bearing, not by the severity of attack. In discussing the mating behavior of wolves, Ginsburg (p. 66) emphasizes the extent and nature of the alpha (highest-ranking) female's limiting influence on the mating activity of the other females. Tinbergen (1965, p. 72) notes the vicious attacks by females on males not in the dominant position. DeVore (1965, p. 286) reports that the female baboon has very definite preferences for her consort, but that she has a great deal less control over the situation than does the female chimpanzee. Beach (1958) cites similar findings with dogs, where females showed strong preferences for certain males and strong dislikes for others which extended over several years. One may also recall Harlow's (1965) emphasis on the unlearned nature of sexually dimorphic behavior in monkey infants (threat, passivity, etc.). Yet, appropriate mounting behavior did not obtain in animals mothered by wire monkeys, and there appeared to be "no adequate innate releasing mechanisms that lead male and female monkeys, regardless of age, to assume normal, effective sexual postures [p. 241]." Harlow's statement has been subjected to question, since the isolation conditions were so severe that they may have greatly upset physiological maturation, and this, in itself, was serious enough to prevent mating.

Beach (1958, p. 272), when discussing the evidence which indicates a direct relationship between hormonal concentration and the display of sexual behavior, insists on the qualification that such relationships do not hold for every female of a species. He points out, as an example, that there are some females that never come into behavioral estrus. "Although the ovaries produce mature follicles which are obviously secreting estrogens and although they show signs of vaginal response to ovarian hormones, there are always a few individuals who fail to display the expected behavioral change [p. 272]." As we ascend the phylogenetic scale, there are indications that among primate females, there are some animals that are totally unreceptive regardless of the state of the ovaries, and there are females that are affected despite the absence of ovarian secretions. The inference is implicit that even among animals phylogenetically lower than man, subtle factors may be influential in sexual behavior, and distinctive preferences may occur so that a given female may be receptive to one male and completely rejecting of another.

Again, before we attempt extensive generalization regarding the hormonal deficits and resultant decrease in sexual behavior which are a consequence of castration, it should be noted that in animals above the level of rodents, the effects of castration vary to a great degree. Male dogs and cats that have had sexual experience retain potency and responsiveness for some time after castration.

This chapter has indicated that with phylogenetic evolution there is increased sexual differentiation and an increasingly proportionate importance given to experiential over hormonal and genetic influences. More important, there are many relevant exceptions to generalizations about animal sex behavior, including wide individual animal variability. Still, the evidence on genetic and hormonal influences implies the need to consider these as potential contributors in reviewing the studies on human behavior, as we will do in the next chapter. We do feel, however, that the complexity and variability of the animal data justifies our opinion that any writer who reads it simplistically may be telling us primarily about his own predilections. Any dogmatic insistence on either the inevitable influence or inevitable lack of influence of the comparative infrahuman evidence is hardly supported by our analysis.

III

The Language of Biology

*I*T IS LIKELY that man's sex role development and sex role behavior are, in part, explicable in biological terms, but the extent to which this is the case is not at all clear. It has been argued that man possesses an inherent somatic sexuality which organizes his psychosexual development. However, it has also been argued that man is essentially psychosexually neutral or undifferentiated at birth, that he is mentally neither male nor female. These arguments define the territory of the present chapter.

The notion that masculinity and femininity have constitutional origins has been accepted for thousands of years. As recently as the last century, major theorists held that there were two basic constitutional types with minor variations. Krafft-Ebing (1922), for example, believed that there were male and female brain centers, though there was little evidence to substantiate this theory. This biological line of reasoning is argued in the more recent work of Broverman and his co-workers (Broverman, Klaiber, Kobayashi, & Vogel, 1968), who maintain that known sex differences in cognitive abilities reflect sex-related differences in physiology. The authors survey evidence indicating that sex differences are reflections of divergencies in relations between adrenergic activating and cholinergic inhibitory neural processes, which in turn are said to be sensitive to the sex hormones, androgens and estrogens. These basic biological gender differences, they say, influence performance of simple perceptual-motor tasks like typing (at which females are superior) and inhibitory restructuring tasks like problem-solving (at which males are superior).

Another presumed demonstration of biological substrata are the studies showing sex differences existing at birth. The work of Moss (1967) with neonates reveals that the sexes possess differential patterns of reactivity at birth, girls being more susceptible to comforting than boys, and mothers, in turn, tending to spend less time nurturing the more irritable males. The relationship between females and mothers is thus more mutually rewarding than that between males and mothers. Several investigators have shown sex differences in neonates, including the demonstration that male infants are, on the average, larger in every dimension and have relatively more muscular development (Garn, 1958), are more active (Knop, 1946), and seem to have a higher pain threshold than do female infants (Lipsitt & Levy, 1959). Garn and Clark (1953) have also shown that males have higher basal metabolism rates than do girls, suggesting different energy levels. A series of studies by Bell (Bell, 1963; Bell & Costello, 1964; Weller & Bell, 1965) indicate that infant females are more reactive to tactile stimulation than are males, and exhibit higher skin conductance.

We proceed now to review briefly other evidence suggesting that genetic and hormonal influences do establish a tendency for sexual behavior and thus for gender role development.

CHROMOSOMAL LEVEL

As a rule, sex determination in higher animals occurs as a result of chromosomal mechanisms. In man, for example, the female normally has two X chromosomes and the male one X and one Y chromosome. Use of new cytological techniques has led to the discovery of abnormal numbers of chromosomes (normally forty-six) in certain individuals. It is only since 1959 that scientists have been certain that the presence of a Y chromosome makes a fertilized ovum develop into a male, and that its absence causes the ovum to develop into a female. Of the twenty-three pairs of chromosomes, only one pair, referred to as the sex chromosomes, determines the child's sex. It was through the efforts of Barr and Bertram (1949), who developed a simple buccal (of the mouth) smear technique, that sex chromatin was shown to be present in female cells and to be absent in male cells. The technique involves microscopic examination of skin biopsy materials, mucosal scrapings, or blood films, and, as Kallman (1963) points out, allows normal individuals to be readily assigned to their correct genetic sex through microscopic determination of their nuclear sex.

Anomalies in sex chromosome structure, due to the loss or addition of a sex chromosome, result in such variants as females who are chromatin-negative and males who are chromatin-positive, when the opposite case (females are chromatin positive) is normal. An example of a chromosomal deviation would be the *Klinefelter's Syndrome*, in which forty-seven chromosomes, including an XXY sex-chromosome complex, are found. An individual possessed of this syndrome is distinguished by small testes after puberty as the most salient feature, and he is sterile. Because of the presence of the male-determining Y chromosome, the individual tends to be phenotypically male, but is also chromatin-positive due to the possession, typically characteristic of females, of two X chromosomes (Barr & Carr, 1960). In *Turner's Syndrome*, there is disturbed sex development in the female as a result of the loss of a sex chromosome (XO). These women are chromatin-negative, have only one X chromosome (Money, 1962), and are characterized by retarded growth, no development of secondary sexual characteristics at puberty (breasts, pubic hair), and intellectual subnormalcy.

Kallman (1963) maintains that the X chromosome is indispensable for fertility in females, while sex determination in males depends on the presence or the absence of the Y chromosome. Thus, irrespective of the number of X chromosomes present, one Y chromosome carries a sufficient number of strongly male-determining genes for male sex determination.

As we have shown in the previous chapter, there is much agreement that animals are subject to inherited tendencies in relation to their sex roles. For humans, the evidence is less compelling. Some of the most relevant work is found in the studies by Kallman (1952a, 1952b), who examined forty pairs of monozygotic twins (identical, having developed from a single fertilized egg) and forty-five pairs of dizygotic twins (fraternal, having developed from two separately fertilized eggs) in which one member of each pair was a known overt homosexual. In the monozygotic twins, he found 100 percent concordance in homosexuality (that is, in all cases where one twin was a homosexual, the other was as well), while for the dizygotic twins, the frequency was similar to that of the general male population. In addition, the mode and extent of deviance were dramatically similar in the monozygotic twins. Kallman concluded that such evidence casts considerable doubt on the validity of purely psychodynamic theories of adult homosexuality. The evidence, he argues, places great weight on genetically determined maleness and femaleness (Kallman, 1952b). Schlegel (1962) examined the histories of 113 pairs of twins and found 95 percent concordance in homosexuality among monozygotic twins and only 5 percent agreement among dizygotic twins, confirming the findings of Kallman.

This brief summary suggests the coercive influence of inheritance

Does it really make a/ difference?

upon the development of sex role. What is lacking is knowledge regarding the mediators of such influence, whether they are genetic effects on the developing central nervous system or hormonal influences.

HORMONAL LEVEL

It has long been known that hormones have significant effects on human behavior. A summary of recent evidence (Hamburg & Lunde, 1966) indicates that the secretion of sex hormones is stimulated by gonadotrophins, which originate in the anterior lobe of the pituitary gland. These gonadotrophins are hormones that prompt development and secretion in the ovaries and testes and regulate the female menstrual cycle. The pituitary action, in turn, is controlled by the brain through the hypothalamus. The onset of puberty apparently involves an interaction between the sex hormones and certain cells of the brain. In normal children, androgenic (male) hormones in the urine occur in almost undetectable amounts until the child's eighth to tenth year of age, at which time the amounts present show a sharp increase in both sexes (Tanner, 1962). Similarly, estrogenic (female) hormones exist in minute amounts in children of both sexes, showing a marked increase at about the eighth or ninth year of age. At this time, the excretion rate of hormones for girls shows a remarkable increase and it becomes cyclic at about the eleventh year, accompanying the acquisition of secondary sexual characteristics and a growth spurt.

A great deal of information regarding the specific influences of the sex hormones on behavior derives from cases in which there exist alterations of the normal state, that is, where hypo- (under) or hyper- (over) function of the endocrines results in abnormal states. These conditions are a result of chromosomal or congenital dysfunctions, and may necessitate surgical removal of the sex glands and hormonal therapy, with significant effects on the individual.

In men the male hormones, androgens, originate in the testes, while in women they derive from the adrenal gland and the ovaries. The bulk of evidence indicates that androgens activate sex drive and that castration or other loss due to some pathological condition reduces sexual impulses, though the latter is directly related to the developmental stage at which castration occurs. The earlier the operation, the more marked the effects on the sexual behavior (Ellis, 1956). Whereas prepubertal castration or removal of the ovaries predictably results in lessened sexual impulse, postpubertal castration or ovariectomy leads to highly variable results. For example, Bremer (1959) and Money (1961a) show that men cas-

trated after puberty continue to have erotic sensations, desires, and fantasies, and do masturbate and occasionally have intercourse. Habits, in the
absence of hormones, presumably can mediate some sexual expression.
However, it should be acknowledged that the absence of androgenic hormones in males does generally lead to a reduction of sexual arousability.
When females are castrated postpubertally, the effects are varied, as in the
study by Filler and Drezner (1944) of forty-one females, where thirty-six
showed no change, three dropped in arousability level, and two exhibited
increased sexual expression. We can see that these varied results travel the
entire range from heightened sexuality to an abrupt cessation of sexual
motivation (Hardy, 1964).

Thus, females, too, are influenced by their endocrines. Several studies (Filler & Drezner, 1944; Waxenberg, 1963; Sopchak & Sutherland,
1960) show the significant role played by androgens in contrast to the
female hormones (estrogens and progesterone) in the activation and
maintenance of erotic feelings and sexual desires in the female. Further,
androgens, which are antagonistic to feminized genital maturation in
women, may be found in excess in some females producing virilizing
hyperadrenocorticism in some girls suffering from this condition (Money,
1961b). These girls have a precocious and exclusively virilizing (masculinizing) puberty. Their ovaries fail to mature and the clitoris becomes
hypertrophied (enlarged) to resemble a penis in size.

As we can see, then, there are some highly dramatic alterations in
sex role behavior that are clinically widespread; these disorders of hormone secretion presumably are initiated by a congenital abnormality, or
hypo- or hyperfunction of the sex glands and the adrenals, which may be
toxically induced, spontaneous, or may derive from several other possible
causes. A ready example is precocious sexual development which involves
the acquisition by a young child of primary and secondary sexual characteristics, including the capacity for ejaculation. Its cause may be a dis-
order of the hypothalamic region of the brain, of the sex glands, or of the
adrenals.

While these examples clearly demonstrate the power of hormonal
factors in extreme cases, they do not tell us what occurs under normal
conditions, and here discussion varies to a greater degree.

In several comprehensive reviews (e.g., Jost, 1958; Burns, 1961),
evidence has been advanced to show that sexual differentiation of the
normal male and female is contingent upon the presence of testicular
substances. If these are present, masculine differentiation occurs; if
absent, feminine differentiation takes place. The mechanism appears to
operate as follows: genetic forces induce gonadal development, and

gonadal development is usually followed by the elaboration of the fetal or neonate gonadal substances responsible for the sexual differentiation of the nervous system (Diamond, 1965, p. 161). It is possible to conclude from this description that at some early point in development where humans are possessed of quantities of hormones of both sexes the human being may be described as a bisexual entity. If one accepts this conclusion, we suggest, however, that in the adult this assumed bisexuality is *unequal* in both the neural tissues and the genital tissues. The capacity exists for giving behavioral responses appropriate to the opposite sex, but the response pattern is variable and, in most mammals that have been studied and in many lower vertebrates as well, the response appropriate to the opposite sex is elicited only with difficulty. It is likely, then, that hormones can be viewed as directional as well as activational, and at birth the individual may be considered to be neurally inclined by genetic and hormonal means toward one sex or the other (Diamond, 1965).

However, there are many subtleties involved in hormonal effects. As was indicated in the previous chapter, recent work with monkeys suggests that the masculinizing effects of male hormones lead to sexual behaviors different from those exhibited by normal females (Goy, 1965; Hamburg & Lunde, 1966). Administering androgens to pregnant females resulted in masculinized female offspring which exhibited behavior more typical of males: threatening, initiating activity, and rough-and-tumble play. Such a relationship between androgens and aggressive behavior may exist in more subtle form in humans. Hamburg and Lunde suggest that androgen effects which take place during critical phases of brain development may influence central nervous system differentiation and the subsequent ease with which patterns of aggression are learned; in addition, large-muscle movements so critical in agonistic encounters might be generally experienced as highly gratifying and therefore be frequently repeated (1966, p. 14), actions intrinsic to the behavior complex referred to as aggression.

To this point, we have examined evidence suggesting the profound influence of genetic and hormonal factors on the development of sex role and behavior. It has been possible to demonstrate with a degree of conclusiveness that in the extreme case, direct outcomes in sex role behavior evolve as a result of genetic and hormonal anomalies. Thus, both seem to provide a powerful influence on sex role behavior and development. Indeed, though more tentative, subtle chromosomal and hormonal forces dispose to alterations in sex role behavior even in the normal developing individual. Though the means of critically determining this latter notion are lacking at present (i.e., we have not the "hardware" necessary), the evidence we do have suggests that many sex behaviors and their correlates

may have their basis in poorly understood chromosomal-brain-endocrine
activities in early, critical periods in development. The argument from the
chromosomal-hormonal position is that inherent sexuality provides a built-
in bias influencing the way an individual interacts with his environment.

*Like
Huff*

EXPERIENCE AND IDENTITY

Now let us turn to an hypothesis counter to the traditional view that
man has inherent sexuality, a position which argues that man is psychosexually neutral, or undifferentiated, with the acquisition of his sex role
contingent upon the particular reinforcements evoked from the environment. This position has been argued since 1955 in the writings of Money,
Hampson, and Hampson. The subjects for their research have been exclusively individuals with morphological incongruities, that is, individuals
like hermaphrodites in whom some contradictions of the biological variables of gender exist. These authors assert that early experience structures
subsequent behavior. According to this theory, termed the "critical period" hypothesis, humans, like other animals, encounter in early development limited and often highly specific periods during which important
social learning takes place, which has a relatively permanent effect on
later social behavior. Supporters of this position contend that certain behaviors receiving reinforcements at brief, early periods in ontogeny become an ineradicable part of the functioning personality (Lorenz, 1957).
In experiments with lower animals, such "imprinting" occurs during a
very short period in development, and its effects are irreversible. Money
(1961a) finds this thesis of great explanatory power in humans, and has
suggested that the critical periods for imprinting gender role in humans
occur during the first two and one-half to three years of life and at puberty. Sex assigned by experience is more crucial to sex role development
than biological sex. In the clinical investigations basic to this position, the
subjects all possessed some contradiction in the six variables of sex. These
six variables are: (1) chromosomal sex, (2) gonadal sex, (3) hormonal
sex, (4) internal accessory organs, (5) external genital appearance, and
(6) assigned sex and gender role. In all cases, in addition, there were
incongruities between somatic and psychosocial factors. Hampson (1965)
points out:

*But
imprinting
implies
some
underlying
biological
mechanism*

> We rather take it for granted that in the ordinary, average human being
> there will be a correspondence between all the variables of sex. That is to
> say, we assume that in an individual with functioning ovaries rather than
> testes, we will find a preponderance of feminizing, estrogen-type hor-

mones, and XX chromatin pattern, the usual female Müllerian derivative, internal accessory sexual structures, typical female external genital structures, and appropriate secondary sexual development. We also expect to find that this person will be living as a woman and will be so classified on her birth certificate. . . . Clearly, study of an individual lacking in a congruence of these indices might shed light on the relative importance of such factors as hormones, gonads, and so on, in the determination of psychosexual orientation and sexual behavior [p. 109].

Hermaphroditic individuals are those in whom exists a contradiction between external genital appearance and sex chromatin pattern, gonads, hormones, or internal reproductive structures. The following case exemplifies the problems confronted by these persons:

> This is the case of an adult woman who was born with masculinized female genitalia, the effects of adrenogenital syndrome (clitoris the size of a small penis and partial fusion of the labia, giving a somewhat scrotal appearance). Her mother was told by the family physician that the infant was a "hermaphrodite," that this meant that it was "not quite a normally sexed female," but that after puberty the surgeons could make it "appear quite normal." She took this to mean that the infant, while mostly female, was also partly male. . . . No one told her the infant was normally female except for adrenals that were pathologically secreting a hormone which masculinzed susceptible tissues. [The child was, as a result, raised ambivalently, though she was a normal female.]
>
> The result in the gender identity of the child and now the adult woman is a fixed sense of being a woman-man who with makeup, shaving, and women's clothes can only masquerade (as she considers it) as a woman. However, she does not feel she is a man and makes no effort to be one. In her daydreams, she at times imagines herself anatomically normal, usually a beautiful woman, rarely a man. She would settle to be unquestionably either but would prefer to be a woman. It is not surprising that she lives a withdrawn life, full of fantasy but with little contact with the world outside her room.[1]

A brief review of some of the studies by Money, Hampson, and Hampson (summarized in Hampson & Hampson, 1961) will afford the reader not only an exposure to the question relating to sex role but also a basis for understanding the position taken by these authors. Over 110

---

[1] Abridged with permission of the author and The Macmillan Company from R. J. Stoller, "The Intersexed Patient—Counsel and Management," in C. W. Wahl, ed., *Sexual Problems: Diagnosis and Treatment in Medical Practice.* Copyright © 1967 by The Free Press, A Division of The Macmillan Company.

hermaphroditic individuals were studied intensively, using clinical interviews, life-data, projective techniques, and observations of mannerisms, demeanor, interests, and so on. The sexual incongruities occurring in hermaphroditism involve some contradictions among the six variables of sex.

1. Chromosomal sex   Twenty patients had been assigned to and reared in a sex contrary to their sex chromatin patterns as established by skin biopsy or the buccal smear technique. Without exception, gender role and orientation as a man or woman, boy or girl, were in accordance with the assigned sex of rearing rather than with chromosomal sex.

2. Gonodal sex   In thirty patients in whom a contradiction was found between gonadal sex and sex rearing, all but three saw themselves in a gender role consistent with their sex of rearing.

3. Hormonal sex   Of thirty-one patients whose sex hormones and secondary sexual body development contradicted their assigned sex and rearing, only five became ambivalent with respect to their gender role. The findings do not offer convincing evidence that sex hormones act as a single causal agent in the establishment of an individual's gender role and psychosexual orientation. The authors observed, "The remaining patients in the group established a gender role consistent with their assigned sex and rearing, despite the embarrassment and difficulties of living with contradictory secondary sexual development [p. 1410]."

4. Internal accessory organs   This sex variable involves the uterus as the organ of menstruation and the prostate and seminal vesicles as organs concerned with the secretion of seminal fluid. In twenty-two of the twenty-five patients, the gender role was concordant with sex of rearing and was not in accord with these predominant male or female internal accessory structures. The authors conclude, "In view of these findings, there seems no reason to suspect any correlation between gender role and the internal accessory organs [p. 1411]."

5. External genital appearance   In the case where twenty-five individuals had been raised in an assigned sex that contradicted their external genital appearance, twenty-three of the subjects had come to terms with their anomalous appearance and had established a gender role consistent with their assigned sex and rearing.

6. Assigned sex and rearing Of the more than 100 cases of hermaphroditism involved in the above findings, in only seven of these cases was there any incongruity between sex of rearing and gender role. The authors conclude with a theme basic to their position, previously stated by Lillie:

> . . . There is no such biologic entity as sex. What exists in nature is a dimorphism within species into male and female individuals, which differ with respect to contrasting characters for each of which in any given species we recognize a male form and a female form, whether these characters be classed as of the biologic, or psychologic, or social orders. Sex is not a force that produces these contrasts; it is merely a name for our total impression of the differences. It is difficult to divest ourselves of the prescientific anthropomorphism which assigned phenomena to the control of personal agencies, and we have been particularly slow in the field of the scientific study of sex characteristics in divesting ourselves not only of the terminology, but also of the influence of such ideas [1961, p. 1430].

In Hampson's words:

> . . . Psychologic sex or gender role appears to be learned, that is to say, it is differentiated through learning during the course of the many experiences of growing up. In place of a theory of innate constitutional psychologic bisexuality we can substitute a concept of psychosexual neutrality in humans at birth. Such neutrality permits the development and perpetuation of many patterns of psychosexual orientation and functioning in accordance with the life experiences each individual may encounter and transact [1965, p. 125].

The "neutrality" position argues that from the moment of delivery when sex determination (via external genitalia) is accomplished, the child's maleness or femaleness is continually reinforced. From that point on, gender role is presumed to be solely the result of learning, regardless of chromosomal, gonadal, or hormonal sex (Money, 1963; Hampson & Hampson, 1961), with the proponents of this theory placing an emphasis on the likelihood of imprinting during critical periods. Thus, sex role development is the predictable result of the particular type of experiences the child encounters. The authors cite as a basis for the imprinting-critical period thesis the particular difficulties in sex re-assignment which occur after three years. What is crucial is that some individuals are raised in a sex role dramatically contradicting their predominant external genitalia, and the accepted gender role is concordant with the sex of assignment rather than the biological sex. Again, the authors' own words succinctly present their position:

> . . . In place of a theory of instinctive masculinity or femininity which is innate, the evidence of hermaphroditism lends support to a conception that psychologically, sexuality is undifferentiated at birth and that it becomes differentiated as masculine or feminine in the course of the various experiences of growing up [Money, Hampson, & Hampson, 1955, p. 316].
>
> Now it becomes necessary to allow that erotic outlook and orientation is an autonomous psychologic phenomenon independent of genes and hormones, and moreover, a permanent and ineradicable one as well [Money, 1961, p. 1397].
>
> It is more reasonable to suppose simply that, like hermaphrodites, all the human race follow the same pattern, namely, of psychosexual undifferentiation at birth [Money, 1963, p. 39].
>
> Thus, in the place of the theory of an innate, constitutional psychologic bisexuality . . . we must substitute a concept of psychologic sex neutrality in humans at birth [Hampson & Hampson, 1961, p. 1406].

In criticizing this position, Diamond (1965) contends that the "neutrality" position is derived from observations of clinical deviations from the normal. Although he did not do so, Diamond might have cited an equally dramatic case exemplifying the opposite effect, described in a recent report by Baker and Stoller (1967). Born and raised as males, five patients showed interest during childhood only in activities typically characteristic of girls. The sixth patient, born and raised a female, had always shown masculine tendencies. All patients possessed normal genitalia at birth and were reared as normal members of their sex. There were no visible anatomical defects present in any of the six until adolescence, when they developed secondary sex characteristics normal for the opposite sex. This pubertal cross-sex bodily change in effect confirmed their earlier gender wishes. It appeared as though the oncoming biological abnormality that was manifested later was latent but still affecting the child's gender behavior from earliest childhood on. The authors concluded that such cases "appear to be exceptions to the general rule that postnatal psychological forces overpower the biological in the development of gender identity [p. 3]."

In general, Diamond asserts that man's behavioral parameters follow the natural scheme of evolution characteristic of all animals, and, since nonhuman species are behaviorally as well as morphologically fixed in a particular sex at birth, the "neutrality" position must therefore argue that man's sexual behavior patterns are basically different from that of animals. This is improbable, says Diamond. Man's sexual behavior is preformed, like that of all other vertebrates subject to prenatally organized mediation, and ontogenetic experiences are *superimposed* (italics our own) on this potentiated nervous system and simply serve to give emphasis and further direction to predisposed tendencies. In addition, Diamond maintains that man's great plasticity in behavior patterns as contrasted with the lower animals' highly stereotyped patterns is consistent with modern genetic and evolutionary concepts. Thus, Diamond's position does not argue against the influence of learning, but instead argues for the interaction of this with genetics. He says:

> Undoubtedly we are dealing with an interaction of genetics and experience; the relative contribution of each, however, may vary with the particular behavior pattern and individual concerned . . . It is the genetic heritage of an individual which predisposes him to react in a particular manner so that the learning of a gender role can occur [1965, p. 158].

Diamond concludes,

> . . . Sexual predisposition is only a potentiality setting limits to a pattern that is greatly modifiable by ontogenetic experiences. Life experiences most likely act to differentiate and direct a flexible sexual disposition and to mold the prenatal organization until an environmentally (socially or culturally) acceptable gender role is formulated and established" [p. 167].

There is no single way to summarize the clash between those who place their greatest emphasis on biological predisposition and those who counteractively emphasize learning and experience as the main factors contributing to sex role development. There is apparently a sufficient variety of abnormal cases at hand to support either position. Unfortunately, while abnormal cases may demonstrate almost anything about abnormal cases, they prove almost nothing about normal development. What we actually witness throughout all human behavior is a fantastic variety in human sexual response, creating the capacity for diverse interpretations. There is no more basis in this material than in that of the previous chapter for simple deterministic accounts formulated in either sociologic or biologic terms. Man appears to be a creature of nature only if society enters into nature's conspiracy, and clearly, we can see that most of the time it does. Though man may be psychosexually malleable, he is not psychosexually neutral.

IV

The Language of Psychoanalysis

*T*HE TRANSITION FROM PHYSICALLY BASED to psychologically based models of sex role development is most readily accomplished through the theory sharing features of both which was proposed by Sigmund Freud. The psychoanalytic approach, heavily grounded in biological concepts, is not only one of the earliest but also one of the most comprehensive psychological theories of personality development. Paradoxically, however, the theory sometimes repels the "scientific" thinker as it excites the "intuitive" mind. Yet, when first outlined it translated into psychological terms personal behavior, drama, literature, and anthropology, making intelligible to psychologists areas previously incapable of being understood. Furthermore, these theorizings have become so much a part and parcel of our culture that although we may be unaware of their influence, few of us are untouched by them. Every time we ponder the reasons for our own or someone else's motivation and fail to be satisfied with a superficial explanation, we are in part revealing this legacy.

Freud was an empiricist and an explorer of unknown territory as well as a constructor of psychological systems. His data was the patient's recall of his own past experiences, a recall which inevitably reflected both the imperfections of the patient's recall and the imperfections of the therapist's memory of that recall at the end of the hour. Clearly, the data of psychoanalysis is hardly suitable for careful scrutiny and objective analysis, yet Freud himself attempted to objectively order his years of observations. While the clinical conditions obviously limited the preciseness and control desired for systematic study, they did afford a representativeness lacking in scientific experiments on human behavior, experiments which

37

by their very nature must be artificial. We deal here only with a selection of Freud's notions of sex role development which have been derived from his complex analysis of psychologic growth.

SEX ROLE DEVELOPMENT

Freud viewed the newborn much as one does the lower animal, that is, as possessed of a reservoir of instincts and instinctive strivings. Each of these strivings has its source in a different bodily region collectively referred to as the *erogenous zones*. An erogenous zone is a part of the skin or mucous membrane which is extremely sensitive to irritation, but certain kinds of manipulation of this zone remove the irritation and produce pleasurable feelings. The lips and oral cavity constitute one such erogenous zone, the anal region another, and the sex organs a third. Sucking produces oral pleasure, elimination creates anal pleasure, and genital pleasure is produced by massaging or rubbing. In childhood, the sexual instincts are relatively independent of one another, but during puberty they tend to fuse together and begin to jointly serve the aim of reproduction.

Freud postulated a *developmental sequence*, a series of stages that all individuals pass through during the first five or six years of life. The stages of development are characterized by the concentration of reaction in a particular part or zone of the body and hence are called the oral, the anal, the phallic-urethral, and the genital stages. Although these phases occur in a fixed sequence, they merge into one another. During the first year of life, for example, the libido (Freud's general term for the life force, a sexual energy) focuses in the oral cavity, and much that is known and experienced is that which is in some way stimulating to the mouth region. After that, the cathexes (attachments) focus in turn on anal gratification, genital gratification, and so on. The ease with which the libidinal needs present at one stage in development are satisfied (for example, by sucking during the oral phase) determines the energy invested in subsequent stages. Frustration during the oral phase may cause a fixation of energies at this level so that lesser amounts of libido can be directed toward anal gratification.

In the course of an individual's development, there is a period, about four to five years of age, in which a large portion of the person's libidinal energy normally becomes attached to the parent of the opposite sex. This leads to what Freud considered one of his outstanding discoveries, the Oedipal conflict, derived from the Greek myth of Oedipus, in which the son Oedipus unwittingly kills his father and later marries his mother, unaware of her relation to him. In childhood, says Freud, sexual feelings are directed toward the mother by the boy, but their expression is blocked by the father and by incest taboos. The father is viewed by the child as all-powerful and he finds intolerable the threat of bodily harm or loss of love from the father for interfering with the mother-father relationship. Through a series of complicated maneuvers, these impulses become repressed into the unconscious in the same way as Freud maintained most undesirable impulses and memories are lost to conscious recall.

During the phallic period, immediately preceding repression of these sexual strivings, the young boy becomes narcissistically identified with his own penis, which is rich in sensation and a source of pleasure. Genital impulses present since birth (but less prominent than oral and anal satisfactions in the early stages) become primary, and simultaneously, the boy experiences the fear of possible loss of the penis or of harm being done to it by his rival father. Freud called this fear specifically the "castration anxiety." As Freud (1948d) stated it:

> The boy retains the same object which he earlier cathected with his pregenital libido. Father appears as a rival he would like to rid himself of and take his place. He makes the assumption that the girl had a phallus which has been cut off because of punishment for inappropriate behavior [p. 189].

It is not felt necessary by psychoanalysts to argue that castration anxiety arises as a result of any actual threats to which the boy is exposed. As Hartman and Kris (1945) suggest, the fear is a natural response to the aggression toward the child by his parents.

> However symbolic or distant from actual castration their threats might be, they are likely to be interpreted by the little boy in terms of his own experiences. . . . That strange phenomenon of a change in a part of his body that proves to be largely independent of his control (the tumescent penis) leads him to react not to the manifest content but rather to the latent meaning of the restriction with which his strivings for mother, sister, or girl playmate meet. And then, what he may have seen frequently before, the genitals of the little girl, acquire a new meaning as evidence and corroboration of that fear [pp. 21–23].

For the girl, this castration anxiety has its counterpart in what Freud termed "penis envy", which occurs when the girl notices the anatomical differences between herself and boys; they have a protruding sex organ, the penis, while she has only a cavity. Presumably, she feels cheated; she would like to have a penis, believing that she once had one but lost it. In her eyes a penis is superior to a clitoris for both masturbatory and urinary functions. Now, it should be clear that these feelings and perceptions described by Freud presumably occur normally in all young boys and girls. It may be clarifying to examine a case in which such feelings are not resolved and have predictive outcomes in the adult personality.

An unsuccessful artist who had always resented being a woman came to treatment very depressed and anxious at having allowed herself to become pregnant. Her husband had recently become extremely successful, and her envy and competition with him were enormous, especially since she was blocked in her own professional development. She felt that the best way to "show up" her husband was to do the one thing he could not do—bear a child.

She expressed only hatred and contempt for her mother, who had been a dependent, ineffectual housebound woman. This resentment seemed to have started at the birth of her sister, three years younger, at which time the patient hid herself and refused to talk for days. The mother, a masochistic woman dependent on her own mother, was hospitalized for depression when the patient was twelve. The father was an unsuccessful artist, an exciting, talented person whom the patient adored. She turned away from her mother and spent the next ten years of her life trying to be her father's son. He encouraged her painting and took her to exhibitions, partly to get away from the mother. However, he was very inconsistent and bitter, given to terrifying rages; he would alternate between leading her on and slapping her down. Her fantasy of being like a boy was brutally crushed at a time when she was preparing for a bas mitzvah; she thought she would be allowed to have one "as good as a boy's" but was suddenly humiliated publicly at puberty and sent home from the synagogue on the Sabbath because it was decided that she was now a woman and could no longer stay and compete with the men and boys. Menarche intensified her resentment of female functions, but she compensated with fantasies of having a son and traveling around the world with him—self-sufficient, no longer needing her family or her father. While in Europe on a scholarship, she fell in love and, while petting with the boy, had the only orgasm she has ever experienced. She feared his increasing power over her, experienced a resurgence of dependency needs and fled home, presumably because her father was ill. She felt she had spent her life trying to win her father's approval. But when she finally had a one-man show, he taunted her, "Why not give it up, go home, and make babies?"

After his death and her professional failure, she became increasingly depressed. At the age of thirty, she decided to get pregnant—after having been married four years. (She had previously been phobic about pregnancy and remained a virgin until her marriage). She felt that her baby was conceived out of emptiness, not fullness, and then feared that the child would take her life from her, would deplete rather than fulfill her. Having a baby trapped her, she felt; she could no longer try to be like a man. It was as though she had had a fantasy penis which she finally had to relinquish.

There was plenty of evidence of typical penis envy in this case. As a girl, the patient even tried to compete with boys in urinary contests, and was furious because she always lost. She first associated her bedwetting with rage at not having a penis, but finally viewed it as a way to punish [her] mother for turning to [the] sister, and as an effort to recover the maternal solicitude she had lost. She envied, and was attracted to, men who had powerful drives for achievement and were free to pursue them. The penis was for her a symbol of such drives; to possess it would also save her from being like her mother. In one sense, she wanted a baby as a substitute for not having a penis; but she also had a burning wish to be a good mother—to prove her own validity as well as to "undo" her past. Her difficulty in achieving this wish forced her to work through her relationship with her mother, which she had contemptuously shelved, finding competition with men more exciting and less anxiety-provoking.[1]

This case depicts the breadth and persistence Freud posited or assigned to crucial psychosexual stages in early life. Clearly, the ramifications of unresolved identity crises during these stages, though complexly transformed, have consequences throughout the individual's history.

In sum then, the whole concept of penis presence or absence is associated with highly involved expectations of self and others, according to Freud. The absence of a penis for the girl is assumed by her to be a kind of punishment which may or may not have been deserved. The boy feels he has something valuable and is afraid he is going to lose it; the girl feels she has lost something valuable already.

It follows that the process of Oedipal activity and its resolution differs for girls and boys. Initially, both sexes identify with the mother as the primary love object, the giver of love and nurturance. Since the boy cannot hope to vanquish the father and win the mother, his sexual wishes for the mother are repressed and he copes with the father by "becoming one with him," that is, by identifying with his father's strength and omnipotence. Masculine behavior develops through this identification with the father figure, which has been described as "identification with the aggres-

---

[1] Abridged from R. Moulton, "A Survey and Reevaluation of the Concept of Penis Envy," *Contemporary Psychoanalysis*, 1970, **7**, 84–104. Used with permission of the author and publisher.

sor (A. Freud, 1946)." As a consequence of this identification, the boy achieves identity with the power represented by the father, and thus vicariously enjoys the mother through the father-mother relationship, which he can now tolerate with little ambivalence. His feeling for his mother is now affection (e.g., tenderness), which is an acceptable emotion.

The events leading to the dissolution of the female Oedipal complex are more devious and involved than those leading to resolution of the male Oedipal conflict. While the boy in the phallic phase remains bound to the mother as was previously the case when she was the object that suckled and nursed him, the girl must exchange her original love object, the mother, for a new object, the father. Although she initially enjoys a close association with and love for the mother, she renounces this parent when she discovers the mother is lacking a penis. Since the mother is seen as responsible for having sent the girl into this world ill-equipped, she transfers her love to the father, who is possessed of the valued organ which she aspires to share with him. Her cathexis for the mother is weakened, and the father is strongly cathected. A brief case history will clarify the issue:

Hilda J. is an 18-year-old girl who was referred to the Psychiatric Clinic because of marked anxiety centering around sexual conflicts involving her relationship with her father. The girl first came to the attention of the authorities eight months earlier when she attempted suicide. At the time she told a story of difficulties at home and of her intense fear of her father. She came to the attention of the police again later when she was arrested for drinking. She showed great anxiety in connection with her father, and told how he beat her and her brothers and sisters, how he drank excessively, and how he attempted to molest her.

When seen at the time of the interview, Hilda was a rather small, thin, dark-haired girl who was pleasant and cooperative, but who obviously was under considerable tension. At the beginning of the interview she pulled at her hands, sighed repeatedly, shifted uncomfortably in her chair, and had difficulty speaking because of her tenseness. The anxiety lessened somewhat in the face of repeated encouragement and reassurance. Eventually she told a story which centered for the most part around her father. She said that he had told her that her mother had frustrated him sexually. At another time he kissed her, but she denied any overt sexual activities with him. She admitted having frequent dreams and nightmares, most of which involved the father. She repeated one dream in which the mother was in the kitchen making supper, and the father tried to get the patient to give him a knife so he could stab the mother. She also had dreams of old men lurking in the street.

Hilda's anxiety became so great that she insisted that her mother sleep with her. Before going to bed, she went through a ritual of barricading the bedroom door, hanging a cloth over the door knob, and forcing the cloth into the keyhole with the point of a butcher knife. She could sleep as long as her mother kept an arm over her, but she awakened and would be terrified when her mother moved her arm away. At the same time, Hilda was frightened by the mother and occasionally hesitated to eat anything the mother had prepared. The girl sometimes was so fearful that she remained awake all night in order to watch her mother.

The most striking element in this case is the dramatic demonstration of the unresolved Oedipal relationship and the anxiety it generated. The problem has been intensified by the father's seductive action toward his daughter and by the passive reaction of the mother to the situation. The girl has deeply ambivalent feelings about both her father and her mother. In spite of her often repeated fear and hatred of the father, she is preoccupied with thoughts of him both in her waking fantasies and her dream life.[2]

In the normal Oedipal resolution, as Freud explains (1948d), "The girl's libido then slips into a new position, one in which she gives up her wish for a penis, and puts in place of it a wish for a child, thus taking the father as a love object [p. 188]." At about age six the girl, as well as the boy, realizes that a desire for the parent of the opposite sex is impossible to gratify. Consequently, she again turns toward the mother; since she cannot afford to lose the mother's love, she relinquishes her incestuous wishes and incorporates the mother image in her own self-concept. The mechanics of incorporation of the like-sex parent for boy and girl are alike. They involve, first, the recognition of the insurmountable barriers to the consummation of the Oedipal wishes due to the mother-father pairing, then, the inhibition or repression of these wishes and the introjection (or taking in) of the feared parent who will not be denied; and finally, identification with that parent, which provides a real sense of "who am I?" for the child.

By identifying with his parents, that is, by endeavoring to mold his own ego to resemble that of the parent who has been taken as a model (Freud, 1949, p. 63), the child begins to acquire some of his parents' personality characteristics, behaviors, and attitudes. Two of the important results of this process of identification are the development of conscience (the superego) and the acquisition of gender-specific behavior and characteristics.

---

[2] From G. W. Kisker, *The Disorganized Personality.* Copyright 1964 by McGraw-Hill Book Company. Used with permission of the author and publisher.

But again, the dynamics of Oedipal resolution differ radically for boys and girls. Whereas for boys the Oedipus complex succumbs to castration anxiety, in girls it is made possible and is led up to by the castration complex. That is, boys see castration as a threat, whereas girls see it as having been carried out (Freud, 1948d, p. 195).

For the boy, the resolution of the Oedipal situation results in the final stages of the development of the superego. The boy is said to "take in" the strength and adequacy of the all-powerful father and to become one with him. This taking in (or introjection) includes the prohibitions and taboos which the father obeys as a member of society. In this way the cultural mores and taboos which society uses as a protection against incestuous activity are incorporated in the young child. His conscience as we know it is established so that he no longer must have recourse to an external agent to judge the goodness or badness of an impulse. Freud (1948d) puts the matter forcefully:

> In boys the complex is not simply repressed, it is literally smashed to pieces by the shock of threatened castration. Its libidinal cathexes are abandoned, desexualized and in part sublimated; its objects are incorporated into the ego, where they form the nucleus of the superego and give that new structure its characteristic qualities. In normal, or rather ideal cases, the Oedipus complex exists no longer even in the unconscious; the superego has become its heir [pp. 196–197].

Unlike that of the boy, the girl's Oedipus complex tends to persist, although it undergoes modification. The repression is never so strong in girls as in boys since the girl's "castration" is completed, the threat is never so intense, and the differences are said to become the basis for many psychological dissimilarities between the sexes that have lifelong consequences. Freud's conceptualization of the girl's resolution of the Oedipal situation strikes one as far more cognitive and incomplete, as though he never fully empathized with nor understood woman as well as he did man. The motive for the destruction of the Oedipal complex in girls is lacking and thus it is only slowly abandoned and may persist for an extended period in the woman's life. As a result, Freud says:

> Their (girls) superego is never so inexorable, so impersonal, so independent of its emotional origins as we require it to be in men. . . . That they show less sense of justice than men, that they are less ready to submit to the great necessities of life, that they are more often influenced in their judgments by feelings of affection or hostility—all these would be amply accounted for by the modification in the formation of their superego which we have already inferred [1948d, pp. 196–197].

And we are now struck by a difference between the two sexes which is probably momentous, in regard to the relation of the Oedipus complex to the castration complex. In a boy, the Oedipus complex, in which he desires his mother and would like to get rid of his father as being a rival, develops naturally from the phase of his phallic sexuality. The threat of castration compels him, however, to give up that attitude. Under the impression of the danger of losing his penis, the Oedipus complex is abandoned, repressed, and in the most normal cases, entirely destroyed, and a severe superego is set up as its heir. What happens with a girl is almost the opposite. The castration complex prepares for the Oedipus complex instead of destroying it; the girl is driven out of her attachment to her mother through its influence of her envy for the penis and she enters the Oedipus situation as though into a haven of refuge. In the absence of fear of castration the chief motive is lacking which leads boys to surmount the Oedipus complex. Girls remain in it for an indeterminate length of time; they demolish it last, and even so incompletely. In these circumstances the formation of the superego must suffer; it cannot attain the strength and independence which give it its cultural significance . . . [1933, p. 129].

In sum, then, Freudian theory organizes the mechanics of sex role identification about the concept of castration anxiety in boys, penis envy in girls, and the Oedipal complex. Between five and ten years of age the child, now possessing some degree of his sex role identity, devotes his energies to other things (school, peers, sex-appropriate activities) and enters what has been called the latency period. He becomes less dependent upon his parents, the ego becomes increasingly the manager of judgment and cognition, the organizer of the personality, and nonlibidinal events claim his primary attention. Infantile sexual interests fade, though the energy available for new attentions and attitudes still derives from a sublimated sexual drive. Much activity involves the strengthening of both ego and superego with continuing introjection of societal mores and rules. In essence, the Freudian model argues for a decline in the strength of instincts with the simultaneous ascendance of ego and superego functions.

Adolescence brings with it a resurgence of energy—and conflicts. Libido is now increasingly concentrated in the genital regions, and the transition to heterosexuality, a change with incumbent problems, becomes the focus of activity (Freud, 1924). Physiological forces reassert their dominance, and the comfortable balance between the ego functions (judging, cognition) and impulses of the id is again disturbed. Behaviorally, the young person turns increasingly to groups and peer relationships in order to inhibit the expression toward the parents of genital impulses which have been tabooed by society. In some measure, Oedipal fantasies are stirred up again and the individual substitutes new love relations for the unattainable goals. Attachments during this phase are uncommonly intense or passionate, and equally quickly abandoned as unsatisfying because they are not the "real" thing.

This, then, in brief, is the basic model of sex role development proposed by the psychoanalytic theory. One gains from it a very real sense of the importance of the physical, erotic, and sensual closeness of children to their parents in this account of sex role. There is nothing here which is impersonal and unseen like chromosomes and hormones. The analysis in this chapter reveals forms of *passion* which, though they have played a vast role in human affairs, seldom find their way into accounts of child development. In pursuit of rigor, some form of emasculation of man as an emotional animal has usually accompanied our traditional science of development, almost as "smashing" in its effects as Freud's description of the development of the Oedipus complex above. There is much data in the psychological literature on infants, children, and other cultures to suggest that Freud's speculations were appropriate to upper-status Viennese living during the late 1800s, but are somewhat less appropriate to the rest of us.

If the framework proposed by Freud strikes us as coherent and sensible, some caution or qualification still seems warranted. Even those who generally subscribe to the Freudian notion of personality development are willing to admit that he tended to underplay the importance of social and economic influences on the family and on individual personality development. Certainly, Freud's analysis of sex role development is conservative, that is, it is a theory which preserves the status quo. In addition, whether intended or not, the concepts can and have been used to justify differing statuses for men and women. Millett (1970) points out its inherent paradox, for although the theory appeared to be a "signal contributor toward softening traditional puritanical inhibitions upon sexuality, the effect of Freud's work was to rationalize the invidious relationship between the sexes, to ratify traditional roles, and to validate temperamental differences [p. 178]."

Freud's training in medicine and biology inclined him toward giving primacy to biological factors in formulating his theory. Thus, the apparent anatomical superiority of the male (in his male-dominated culture of the late 1800s) became Freud's foundation for developing a complex psychological structure. In particular, Freud assigned women a position of biological inferiority because of their lack of a penis. In addition, he insisted that the young girl should recognize that its possession provides a superior status (whether for urinary or masturbatory purposes). Thus, by definition, he made the penile homologue (the clitoris) inadequate, and claimed the young girl felt cheated and punished by the lack of a penis. From this basic assumption, the whole counteractive series of episodes which ultimately provides the feminine sex role is said to have emerged. That is, much of feminine psychology can be understood as a reaction against the presumed deficit, the lack of a penis. This premise, at best, ignores the cultural context in which Freud's own theories evolved, and markedly ignored far more tenable notions regarding the equation: femininity = inadequacy. It must be apparent that we have no precise or universally applicable data on the age at which the penis becomes important, nor do we really know all the possible varieties of reactions to its importance that occur, on the part of males as well as females. One can certainly question whether the female's early recognition of her own lack of a penis is, in fact, as catastrophic an event as Freud supposed. Millett (1970) provides her most damning criticism of Freud when she adds that he fails to note the fact that "woman is born female in a masculine-dominated culture which is bent upon extending its values even to anatomy and is therefore capable of investing biological phenomena with symbolic force [p. 180]." Clearly, social explanations for the disadvantaged position of the female in a male-dominated culture make greater sense in developing the psychology of femininity than does the appeal to tenuous embryological and anatomical sources. Still, while acknowledging the correctness of her criticisms of Freud, we can see a certain arrogance in some of the current usages of historical hindsight, as when Millett says, "Freud appears to have made a major and rather foolish confusion between biology and culture, anatomy and status [p. 187]."

From our present historical position, then, and benefiting from generations of Freudian-type psychogenic thinking, we can agree that there is something of a compensatory "masculine" ring to Freud's whole theory with its emphasis on the primacy of the penis. On the other hand, one should not be blinded to the herculean task Freud performed of relating the complex genesis of morphology, social status, and psychological dynamics that he more aptly described and communicated than had anyone else up to that time. Nor can one ignore the most comprehensive theory of the genesis of sex role development thus far provided us simply because some ingredients of that framework appear to be somewhat less tenable today than when they were formulated. Freudian thinking admixed the complexes of biology, socialization, and family dynamics to provide insights which have persisted, not so much because of their "exciting" nature as because they order, integrate, and make sense of a bewildering assortment of contributions to human behavior. That is to say, the language of psychoanalysis undoubtedly provides a sufficiently comprehensive framework with relevant parameters of human activity to communicate to the reader of that language an understanding of some of the more complex aspects of human life.

Whether or not Freud really understood the psychology of women is another question, though a related one. From his perspective as a man and as a member of a culture dominated by men, he constructed the dynamics of women as a counterpart to the masculine role of the times. It is thus not surprising that one has the feeling that although Freud had much to say about the "unconscious," females still remained something of a mystery for him within his theories, as they were within his own life. Freudian psychology was also Freud's own psychology. Indeed, though he constructed a complex system interpreting the psychology of women, in a moment of exasperation he once said, "The great question that has never been answered and which I have not been able to answer, despite my thirty years of research into the feminine soul is 'What does a woman want?' [E. Jones, 1953, Vol. II]."

The point for our purposes must be that just as no adequate account of sex and identity can ignore aspects of the language of genetics, hormones, and morphology, neither can such an account ignore the language of human passion. Whether or not the Freudian language is the most appropriate example is another question.

V

The Language of
Social Learning Theory

THE INITIAL EFFORTS to apply learning theory principles to personality development emphasize some rules provided by Pavlov, Hull, and others, derived from the way in which animals learn in highly controlled situations. These ventures were not generally held to be effective in accounting for the development of complex social behavior and led ultimately to a less restricted model emphasizing social learning and imitation (Dollard & Miller, 1950; Rotter, 1954; Skinner, 1953; Mowrer, 1960; Bandura & Walters, 1963; Mischel, 1966).

SOCIAL LEARNING THEORY: ITS BASIC ELEMENTS

Social learning theory is grounded in two major streams of psychological thought: S-R (stimulus-response) theory and psychoanalysis. Basically, it is a theory of social learning and socialization in the child originally inspired by psychoanalytic concepts but which translates causal explanation into S-R terms. As Baldwin (1967) notes in his summary of its development:

> . . . Social learning theory began as a psychoanalytically inspired S-R theory of development of the child's social relations and personality. However, the findings of empirical research have lead to revisions of the theory and have posed problems which are not rooted in psychoanalysis [p. 438].

How does the socialization process occur? According to social learning theory, very early in life the child becomes psychologically dependent on the mother for total care and sustenance. The child sees the mother as the one who takes care of him, doing those things that make him comfortable. The constant association of the mother's presence with comfort and satisfaction as opposed to the association of frustration and discomfort with her absence leads the child to value mother-presence and experience anxiety in her absence (dependency anxiety). Thus, by the end of the first year of life, the child has learned the value of maternal approval-disapproval, or more strictly, the mother's behavior has become an effective reinforcer for the child. Usually this is followed by the mother increasing her expectations and demands. The child thus learns to perform additional actions that will bring this approval. According to this theory, the mother's behavior is the crucial element in fostering the dependency that, in turn, leads the child to become increasingly responsive to the direct reinforcements of other persons. This dependency generalizes to others, making the child subject to the responses and rewards of the other significant persons. The controlling element in the degree of learning on the part of the child is the balance of reinforcements administered. But the theory is not so naive as to argue that every response needs to be reinforced in order for the behavior to be acquired. The principle of generalization can account for the learning of some behaviors that have not previously been reinforced. This principle holds that when a response has been learned to one stimulus, that response is likely to be evoked in the presence of stimuli that are psychologically and physically similar to the original stimulus. Generalization accounts for the child's response to adults (parent-surrogates) in terms of the responses learned earlier in relation to his own parents.

Basically, then, this is learning in relation to another person, that is, social learning. Although learning which occurs in the early months of life is considered to be readily accounted for by the traditional principles of administered rewards and punishments, as the developing child becomes increasingly aware of the dispensers of rewards and punishments as social objects, a new and more complex form of learning involving imitation and modeling of these social objects becomes available to him and becomes more effective than simple reinforcement. This higher form of learning entails the acquisition of larger patterns of responses rather than just the isolated elements (bits) that are rewarded. Learning may occur through observation of the behavior of others, even when the observer does not reproduce the model's behavior during learning and is not directly reinforced by an adult for showing the behavior at a later time. After infancy most children develop a generalized habit of matching the responses of successful models, models such as the mother and father. It is contrary to classical S-R principles that learning, such as imitation learning, can occur in the absence of reinforcement and drive reduction. In the traditional learning schema, some consummatory act must occur (e.g., eating when hungry) in order for something to be learned. In this higher form of learning, such drive reduction is not necessary for the acquisition of a response. According to social learning theory, social behavior is acquired more rapidly than is acknowledged by classical S-R theorists, who would propose an administered reinforcement schedule.

The manner in which social learning theorists have come to treat the development of aggressive responses in children illustrates the shift toward modeling explanations. In the past it was thought necessary that the child be frustrated in order to make him behave in a manner labeled aggressive, and to have this behavior rewarded or inhibited to perpetuate or to eliminate it. But there has accumulated much evidence indicating that it is mainly imitation of the aggressive behavior in the models which results in aggressive behavior in the child. Even when there is the verbal prohibition of aggressive behavior by a model who is displaying aggressive behavior, the child may still display aggressive behavior. The adult's negative reinforcement is less effective than the model provided by his own behavior, for children tend to imitate what he practices rather than what he preaches. Thus, many aggressive actions may be acquired in circumstances that do not involve frustrations or anger. Of course, in life the learning of such behavior is more complex than this explanation would suggest. Whether aggression is expressed in a situation also depends on the extent to which such behavior is reinforced or inhibited in such a situation. Parents are more likely to reinforce what are called aggressive responses when they are directed toward others rather than to the self or the parents. Furthermore, if a male is exhibiting such behavior, he is more likely to be reinforced than would be a female. This example clarifies the unique contribution of social learning theory in its departure from traditional S-R notions. The child, merely by observing the model, may infer reinforcement consequences. He need not perform the behavior at that time, for he is capable of retaining it symbolically (concept formation, words) and of employing these unpracticed behaviors at a later time when such behavior is either appropriate or likely to be reinforced.

In traditional learning theory, man as well as animals was viewed as an organism which was the *passive* recipient of alternations of external rewards and punishments. Principles of contiguity and frequency of reinforcement were said to modify behavior in the direction of that which was to be learned. In social learning theory, the observer is clearly a more active participant, either through direct or covert modeling.

Another concept used in social learning theory is identification. Freud (1925) introduced the term very early in his theory of psychoanalysis to explain the capacity of the organism to learn and incorporate characteristics of the parents in the course of socialization. Despite the varied use of the term as an explanatory concept (Sanford, 1955; Kagan, 1958; Sears, 1965; Bronfenbrenner, 1960), identification is usually employed to categorize remarkably complex and elaborate behaviors for which direct tuition (i.e., rewards and punishments) has not been provided, for which no obvious motive to learn exists in the child, and yet, that come to be a part of the child's behavior.

Learning theorists have argued that this identification is, in essence, no different than imitation.

> . . . Observational learning is generally labeled "imitation" in experimental psychology and "identification" in theories of personality. Both concepts, however, encompass the same behavioral phenomena, namely the tendency for a person to reproduce the actions, attitudes, or emotional responses exhibited by models [Bandura & Walters, 1963, p. 89].

In disagreement with this, some students of socialization suggest that:

> . . . It is generally used to denote a particular kind of imitation: the spontaneous duplication of a model's complex, integrated pattern of behavior (rather than simple, discrete responses), without specific training or direct reward but based on an intimate relationship between the identifier and the model [Mussen, 1969, p. 718].

In this latter view, identification refers to the situation where a child acquires as his own the behaviors of another because he would (if he had the choice) be like the model with whom he identifies.

In summary, according to social learning theory the basic progression of the child is from the role of dependency in infancy, through the development of dependency anxiety, to the gradual translation of innate and acquired behavior dispositions into acceptable adult forms brought about through reinforcement, fear of punishment, and the mechanisms of imitation and identification.

THE DEVELOPMENT OF THE SEX ROLE

According to social learning theory, masculinity and femininity are not simply the result of birth as a boy or a girl. The gender role is assigned to the child at this time based on his biological sex, and he is subsequently treated as a member of that sex. In accord with cultural prescription regarding the manner in which boys or girls are viewed, different attitudes are evidenced toward children of different sexes, and different behaviors of these children are reinforced. A set of rules is established for the child which is based on his sex (his sex role), and the aim of the parent is to provide those reinforcements which conduce to the adoption and assimilation of that role. Sears (1965) says, "Once society has agreed on a gender label, the gender-appropriate forms of behavior must be learned by the child [p. 133]." Implicit in the above statement is the idea that there is nothing inherent in the child that in absence of reinforcement will give rise to sex-appropriate behaviors as prescribed by society. Hence, appropriate sex role development presumably results from sex designation at birth and the subsequent imposition on the child of a number of training practices and modeling experiences that are intended to result in shaping his behavior so that specific masculine or feminine qualities will emerge.

Unfortunately, this account overlooks many complexities. There are a number of sources of variability that may disturb any possible homogeneity in sex role learning. Cultural ascriptions to sex role are not necessarily clear and unchanging. They may vary as a function of culture, and certainly as a function of subcultural expectations within the same society. For example, in the expression of aggression, differences in sex role expectations are found among the lower and middle classes in our own culture, with greater freedom allowed in the lower socioeconomic group than in the middle group. Additionally, parents and peers evidence a great variety of expectations regarding the qualities expected of an individual. Lastly, the nature of masculinity and femininity involves a highly complex set of personality variables, not completely understood or delimited. In the behavioral repertoire of both boys and girls are dispositions to respond to similar situations in fashions that are not gender-specific. There continue to be numerous situations at various developmental levels in which male-female responses are not clearly differentiated (e.g., male and female vocational pursuits), and consequently there are some classes of behavior and preferences that do not readily fit role expectations.

Notwithstanding these comments, though, sex role development does take place to a satisfactory degree in the majority of individuals. The child does learn that appropriate sex role behaviors are those for which only one sex is typically rewarded. In so brief an examination of the learning of sex role, one must qualify the generalizations offered. For example, intuitive-feeling behavior may be viewed as present in both sexes, though categorized as sex-appropriate for females in our culture. As a result, such behavior is encouraged (that is, reinforced) in females, while we fail to reinforce it in males. At the same time, the conditioning of such behavior in males is not necessarily aversive. Rather than a simplistic explanation, it is far more likely that these behaviors are rewarded with different fre-quency for each sex, and thus, each sex tends to display such behaviors with different frequencies. Sex-inappropriate behavior, on the other hand, is likely to be punished and hence to diminish in strength and frequency (Mussen, 1969, p. 713).

When we move beyond this general level of treatment it is important to realize that social learning predictions are meant to be made only in terms of the history of the individual organism. In any situation, there are a number of responses available to the individual, each of which may be seen as possessing a particular probability of occurrence dependent upon the previous learned consequences (i.e., reward for sex appropriateness) of that response in that situation. While responses appropriate to one's sex are most likely to bring approval and are thus most likely to be emitted, it is not enough to suggest that since aggression, for example, is most fitting for the male sex role, every male will be consistently more aggressive than every female. Knowledge of each situation and its probable outcome is necessary for predicting individual behavior, to account for variability in an individual's responses across situations. Aggressiveness has different probabilities of occurrence toward specific classes of objects, but a prediction requires knowledge of the specific situation and specific object to increase its precision. Though aggression toward females is less likely in males than is aggression toward other males, it is less apt to be directed toward older women or mother-surrogates, and far more apt to be directed toward tomboyish females in late childhood or adolescence. We are saying then, that sex differences may be generalized, but prediction of individual behavior requires further knowledge of specific situations and conditions. In addition, certain behaviors are reinforced for either sex, while certain others are differentially reinforced contingent upon the age of the responding person. For example, dependency is sanctioned for both sexes in early childhood, and thereafter decreasingly reinforced for boys as a function of age. As evidence of this, children feel their parents show, in increasingly obvious ways, that they want their children to adopt appropriate sex role behavior (Fauls & Smith, 1956), and fathers admit desiring their growing sons to behave in expected sex-appropriate ways (Aberle & Naegele, 1952). On the other hand, where aggression is negatively sanctioned for females in general, during early adulthood such behavior is approved when coordinated with independence and autonomy in job-seeking.

In sum then, the social learning theory of sex role development tends to emphasize differential employment of rewards and punishments

contingent upon the child's sex. The processes considered in social learning theory are based on this manipulation of punishments and rewards,
which produces sex-appropriate behavior within the context of social
agents (family, friends, or peers), with subsequent generalization of this
learning in response to others. The adoption of sex-appropriate behavior
is reflected in the increased frequency with which such behaviors occur in
the repertoire of the boy or girl. Following this initial learning, a new and
more powerful method of acquiring sex role occurs through imitation
learning, which is simply the observation of an appropriate model's behavior resulting in the acquisition of additional and complex behavior patterns. Apparently, imitation learning does not require the child to perform
the learned behaviors immediately or to receive reinforcement of these
new behavior patterns. Finally, the most complicated sex-appropriate patterns of behavior are gained by the developing child without evident reinforcement by other agents, which has led social learning theorists to
posit the mechanism of identification, termed identificatory learning,
which implies that the child develops a drive or motive to be like a model,
typically the parent of the same sex. This particular explanatory concept is
usually employed to account for the acquisition of complex, integrated
patterns of sex role behavior which were not preceded by any specific
training or tuitioning. As certain learning theorists (Mussen, 1969;
Kagan, 1958) have suggested, identification occurs in the context of an
intimate, satisfying relation between subject and model, with the resulting
sex role identification a stable and enduring outcome of such identificatory
learning.

LIMITATIONS OF THE MODEL

Though the proponents of social learning theory are characterized by
the rigor in their thinking, there are obvious limitations in their manner of
describing those events which lead to normal sex role identity. One of the
difficulties in the system is the unrelenting demands the experimenter
makes upon himself with his rejection of other strategies of gaining information. For example, most of the social learning research involves only
manipulative studies in the laboratory and avoids field studies, case studies, and naturalistic observation as means of testing hypotheses. Baldwin
(1967) provides a telling criticism of the system when he suggests that it
was developed:

. . . to explain the acquisition of behavior rather than the actual events
that take place between stimulus and response. Every theory of human

behavior must contain both a theory of action which describes the process by which behavior at the moment is elicited and carried out, and a theory of acquisition which describes the temporal sequence of events resulting in the formation of various kinds of dispositional variables [p. 485].

Commonly found, then, is the criticism that social learning theorists study only those behaviors that can be systematically reinforced. The learning theorist cannot be certain that the behavior he studies is *typical* of the organism's repertoire of response, he only knows that it is present and can be modified under certain conditions. Nor can he be certain that his experimental reinforcements are comparable to the natural reinforcers existing in the organism's normal environment.

Having made these criticisms, it still must be conceded that learning theorists have contributed considerably to our understanding of the ways in which behavior is shaped in certain directions and why some behaviors are amplified and some are diminished. Parents, society, and culture clearly benefit from producing children with certain "acceptable" characteristics, and the language of learning theory describes with some adequacy how they achieve this end. What we have to watch is that the results of these studies be treated only as samples contained within the normal limitations of time and not as yielding universal and enduring information about sex differences. It is common to find that the descriptions by those who employ the languages of psychoanalysis and social learning of boy-girl differences are treated not as the moments in cultural history that they are, but as "universal" almost "instinctive" statements about sex differences.

VI

The Language of Sociology

WE MOVE NOW from the study of biological and psychological man to the social context in which he is embedded. Sociological conceptions of development are those theories in which the primary focus is on the social system and its effects on parent-child relationships as the major influence in individual development; child-rearing practices are said to present merely one aspect of the functioning of a social system. The tendency in sociology is to view the parent-child relationship (which is central to social learning theory) only in the context of the larger society, for it is the functions of the society that are served by child training. This viewpoint is expressed in what we know as role theory and social system theory which, unlike traditional social learning theory, focuses its approach on interpersonal or interactional relations, and places a greater emphasis on cognitive learning. The special concern on the range of parent-child interactions is with the *mutuality* of effects, rather than merely one-way effects. The basic unit of analysis, then, is normally the group or institution, and the focus is less on the individuals who comprise the group than on the structure of their relationships.

In the following discussion, the elucidation of sex role development from the sociological point of view will rest most heavily on the writings of a few men who have investigated child development problems and incorporated them into the body of sociological theory. The writings of Talcott Parsons (1942, 1964), Orville Brim (1957, 1958, 1960), Robert Bales (1950), Parsons and Bales (1955), and Parsons, Bales, and Shils (1953) provide the major substance of this discussion. Parsons, in particular, has attempted to develop a general theory of human action capable of accounting for the development of individual behavior while at the same time coping with the problems of the social system.

In order to set the groundwork for the sociologic model of sex role development, some general introductory remarks must be made regarding the nature of the social system in which child development and role construction are incorporated.

Parsons and Bales (1955) generally accept the correctness of the psychoanalytic approach, but supplement this with an analysis of the changes in the growing child's role in the family, giving their emphasis to the dynamics of family interaction that provide the actual socializing influence upon the child. They consider the psychoanalytic conception of parent-child relationships a somewhat static view. Though Freud developed the notion of the importance of the complex of family factors (persons and characteristics) which contributed to the personality development and, in particular, the sex role development of the child, he tended to assign to those members archetypal-like characteristics, as though the basic family members were but carriers of qualities which transcended time and conditions. Parsons, on the other hand, insists that each generation and each particular family within each culture provide unique qualities which emerge in the course of their interaction over time, such that each member exerts an interactive, shaping influence on all other members. This latter conception provides a basis for variability and change that appears to be absent in the psychoanalytic model. Furthermore, where the social learning psychologist looks for causal bases to explain the emergence of certain types of mechanisms and behaviors in the child (e.g., the effects of particular child-rearing practices on personality development of the child), sociologists argue that some of the causal links, presumably parent-directed-to-child, are, in fact, parental adaptations to the child's behavior and cognitions. That is to say, they argue that either the parent's or the child's behavior can be understood only by knowing the effects of others on him, and the effects of his behavior on them. The mother and the infant are a mutually responding pair, with the behavior of one affecting the other, and these two form a system which involves all participants. In addition, every social system, such as this parent-child system, has certain *functions* which it performs for society in general. The societal function of the parent-child system is physical care and training of the child so that he becomes a suitable member of the society, both as a child in the child role and as an adult in the adult role. The social system, according to Parsons, can only be maintained through this process of socialization. Though the function of the family in a complex society such as ours is not to be interpreted simply as carried out on behalf of society, human personality must nevertheless be made suitable for society through the socialization process. Certain practices must be employed to produce adults who fit into the existing role system, or the society will disintegrate or change. Therefore, the central focus of socialization lies in *the internalization by the child of the cultural norms of the society into which he is born* (Parsons & Bales, 1955, Ch. 1, italics added). The family is seen as containing four kinds of status roles: the individual's position is differentiated by generation (parent-child) and differentiated by sex (male-female). The father role is, relative to the others, high on power and instrumentality, but low on expressiveness. The mother role is high on power and expressiveness, and low on instrumentality. The instrumental-expressive distinction, according to Parsons, is an essential differentiation of function found in all group life. By *instrumental* he refers to the pragmatic concern for the relations between the system and the outside world (e.g., goal orientation). By *expressive* he refers to concerns with the internal affairs of the system, the maintenance of integrative, harmonious relations between the members (Parsons & Bales, 1955). Parsons (1964) sees the nuclear family as a special case of this basic four role pattern, with generation as the main axis of superior-inferior, or leader-follower differentiation (in all groups), and sex as the main axis of the instrumental-expressive differentiation. He argues that there is no known system that fails to discriminate the four cardinal roles in the nuclear family (p. 60). Parsons cites as evidence Zelditch's (1955) study examining seventy-five primitive societies, in which Zelditch found an overwhelming preponderance of relative instrumentalism in the father role; in no case was the mother's role more instrumental than that of the father. In this light we can connect instrumental cultural behaviors with the father role and expressive cultural behaviors with the mother role.

SEX ROLE AND ITS IMPORTANCE

The basis for this allocation of roles between the biological sexes, discussed by Parsons, is the fact that the bearing and early nursing of children makes primary the relation of the mother to the small child (expressive-within-system function). This, in turn, establishes a presumption that the man, who is exempted from these biological functions, should specialize in the alternative instrumental (between-systems) direction (Parsons & Bales, 1955). In his conceptual framework, Parsons employs as an example a family prototype which is composed of a father, mother, son, and daughter. He maintains that the differentiation of sex roles within the family constitutes not merely a major axis (along with age and generation) of its structure, but sex is also deeply involved in both of these two central function-complexes of the family. That is, the functions necessarily served by any group are, in part, an extension of the biological requirements of males and females. The importance of the family for society rests on this social necessity rather than on it being a unit purely reproductive in function.

It should be noted that Parsons views personality and sex role development as evolving in four major phases, which show a high degree of correspondence to the stages of psychosexual development described by Freud. However, these stages (oral, anal, phallic, and genital) offer, in addition, major phases of increasing social control, interaction changes, and differentiation. Each of the phases provides evidence of a previously stable state, and with the change, a period of integration into a new "plateau" occurs. The first phase is the *oral dependent* phase, in which the child forms an attachment to one or a class of social objects of which the mother is the prototype, and the major gratifications of the ego are fused to these objects. In this system, the mother plays all those roles associated with power, and the child remains the undifferentiated and passive recipient of her nurture. This phase (system) remains relatively stable until the attainment of a new level of control, and the child enters the so-called *anal stage*, which is described by Parsons as a period of sphincter-control allowing increasing autonomy in interaction with the mother. Here the child differentiates himself from the mother, and the relationship truly becomes a dyadic one. The mother is perceived as powerful and adaptive (instrumental) in relation to the child (i.e., she is concerned with solving external problems).

These first phases for both the boy and girl have the function of integrating the child into the family as a wider operating unit. The use of rewards and punishments with the child brings about internalization of the value patterns prevalent in the family as a system. Parsons contends that while children of both sexes start life with essentially the same relationship to the mother, at some point in development the boy must learn to differentiate himself from the mother and "identify" with the father, just as the girl must learn to identify with her mother. Both parents usually expect this. The reciprocal love attitude between child and mother is the initial condition. The child is at first dependent upon the mother for most sources of gratification, this dependency tends to increase with time, and the child's expectancies regarding the mother are increasingly established. As Parsons (1964) notes, "her [the mother's] behaviors are translated into *signs* of what she expects of the child, and the erotic contactual relation becomes a focus on her attitudes which is expressed by the eroti-

cally pleasurable stimulation her contact and constancy affords [p. 27]."
This results in need satisfactions, and, in addition, there emerges a complex language of emotional communication between child and mother.
Ultimately, however, this gratifying love relationship with the mother
must be renounced, the child becoming less mother-centered and more
family-centered. Parsons (1964) notes that in the kinship system, the
marital relationship ultimately takes precedence over the mother-child
relationship (p. 38). Therefore, we can see that there is some conflict for the
developing child regarding the position of the father. This is resolved
when *both* parents emphasize that the child renounce his dependence on
the mother. The father's intrusion into the mother-child relationship
brings a responsibility to the child for being independent and for making a
realistic appraisal of his inability to gratify erotic attachments. In these
circumstances, the father is viewed ambivalently, for the child's perception
mixes hostility with respect and awe.

It is during the period of the child's differentiation from the mother
that the former begins to learn roles and gain some predictive knowledge
regarding the nature of the social system. Baldwin (1967), in reviewing
Parsons, interprets this phase as one in which love-dependency emerges,
contrasting with the caretaking-dependency which previously characterized the interaction system. Giving and withdrawing love (which is the
mother's principal power at this stage) shapes the autonomy and the role
of the child; that is, he learns not only his role, but that of the mother. The
next phase comes about as a resolution of the Oedipal crisis wherein, it
will be recalled, the child develops a conscience representing the voice of
the father through which the values of culture are transmitted. Here we
find the transition from a dyadic system (mother-child) to the quadratic
(four-person) system of the nuclear family (mother, father, child, sibling). According to Parsons, the outstanding feature of this period in the
child's development is his establishment in the basic social system of the
nuclear family. Autonomy is displayed not only in relation to the mother,
but also in relation to the father and the sibling. Though this is seen as an
integrative period, the father appears as a new and significant element
introduced into and altering the system, a figure instrumental in character
who imposes new demands upon the child through his role as disciplinarian and with his increased demands for an achievement orientation on
the part of the child. The mother thus relinquishes to the father the
instrumental role she has played for the child and becomes primarily
expressive in her relationships with him. That is, the mother retains her
role as integrator and conciliator, while the father takes on the role of
decision maker, disciplinarian, and so on.

This phase also involves the internalization of the sex role. It is fundamental in the child's development for it provides the first real differentiation of family roles that transcend the family and "become constitutive of the larger social structure [Parsons, 1964, p. 42]." Father, representing for the boy the prototype of adult masculinity, and for the girl the masculine counterpart of mother's femininity, is crucial in the learning of role differentiation in the family. In addition, the role characteristics presented presumably have their counterparts in all social systems.

In moving from the earlier dyad to the new quadrad, the boy starts with an identification with the mother which ultimately expands to include the whole family. In addition, he acquires a sex role identification with the father. For the girl, a "direct apprenticeship" in the adult female role through imitation of the mother is continually available. The process is less erratic than that of the boy since she continues the initial identification, while the boy must imitate the less available father. It is natural that the girl shall identify with the mother in early life, but the boy soon learns from his parents' attitude the unacceptability of continuing to model feminine behavior. The new male role involves elements which thus appear, at times, less natural than compensatory. That is to say, in some ways the boy is absorbing the masculine role as a defense against continuing to play the feminine role rather than experiencing the masculine role as a source of positive identification.

Parsons makes clear that as important as Freud's theory of psychosexual development is, he failed to note the decisive consequences of the total social system upon the sex role identity of the child. The father is more than the competitor and the feared antagonist crucial to the resolution of the Oedipal crisis. He is also a part of a social collectivity which the developing child wishes to emulate. These dynamics of family interaction result in the extension of the child's reference system outside the family into the greater society. The building of universalistic patterns of orientation, especially learning to value achievement and acceptance of the discipline necessary for developing technical skills requires release from too intense an involvement with erotic attachments. If we consider the psychosexual development in this way, the steps appear to be first bringing the child into the total family on a responsible level, and forcing him to relinquish erotic priority of the mother-child relationship to the marital relationship. Next, he is categorized by his sex and is motivated to adopt a whole pattern of behavior appropriate to his gender which serves to bring him for the first time into equivalence with persons outside the family (i.e., boys and girls of his age level). School activities further accentuate this experience. It is only after sufficiently strong character structure develops in these other respects (during the latency period) that he is again permitted erotic attachments (genitality), this time outside the family and with a fundamental alteration in role structure with the child readily assuming the parental role type. As Parsons points out, a boy does not become his father, nor does he take over his place, but becomes a *father* in his own new family. That is to say, part of his identity is achieved through elements particular to his own father. But more important, through this identification he learns the generalized *role* of the man and the father common to our culture. In turn, a girl does not take her mother's place with the father and siblings, but becomes a mother and wife outside the family orientation. Sex role development then involves the specifying of a *generalized* sex role type which has been learned. That is to say, the boy internalizes a generalized role pattern for "man" consisting of the qualities and behaviors exemplified by the adult male. Identification according to Parsons is therefore somewhat different from identification defined by the Freudians. Identification cannot mean coming to be the object, but is an internalization of a common culture, or the incorporation of it into the actual structure of the personality.

In sum, the father breaks up the early mother-dependency and motivates the child to an achievement-oriented performance, and his role model functions in connection with the attainment of sex role for the boy, and serves as the ideal of masculinity for the girl. This acts as a bridge to the patterning of orientation toward the primary extrafamilial (universalistic) values and roles (Parsons, 1964, p. 47).

The substance of Parsons' theory of sex role development presented here should enable us to recognize this as a traditionalist theory, one placing primary responsibility for socialization as well as for sex role development on the influences within the family. Here, the family is conceived of as a microcosm of the greater system (society), and its structures and activities, though paralleling the larger system, occur primarily on its own behalf. Notwithstanding the potency and durability of such learning in early life, his theoretical position gives little emphasis to primary socializing institutions supplemental to the family, such as peer group influences, or to those individuals influential in the course of school experience. Orville Brim has dealt with these factors (1957; 1958; 1960).

Brim argues that if socialization is viewed as role learning, it must occur throughout an individual's life, well beyond the early years. As a result, the acquisition of the content of one's sex role is a persisting, ongoing life process influenced by peers, teachers, and others. The individual's sex role demands different responses from him at different times in his development; consequently, he is constantly comparing his own performance in his sex role with the expectations he perceives others hold for him, or which he holds for himself because of earlier learning (e.g., what his parents might expect of him).

Social role learning occurs as a result of continued participation in interaction situations with others, this interaction thereby providing the individual the opportunity to practice his own role as well as to take the role of the other (Brim, 1958). Brim contends that the process of role acquisition involves learning the behaviors appropriate to a position in a group through interaction with others who hold *normative beliefs* about what this role (e.g., as a male) should be and who are able to reward and punish the learner for correct and incorrect actions. Stated in another fashion (Cottrell, 1942), interaction between two persons leads to the assimilation of roles, to the incorporation of elements of the role of the other into the actor's role. Thus, the developing child learns the gender role appropriate to him by interacting with members of both sexes. His daily experience provides interaction with peers and adults who demand of him that he discriminate between them, that he behave in different ways toward them, and that he develop the desire to do so (Brim, 1960).

Many essays (though not so much research) have been written on the role of the school in maintaining the sex role dichotomy. It has been suggested that in America the high percentage of women in the teaching role in elementary school keeps the boy in a tutelage to women that he is eager to escape. Education itself becomes confused with maternal dependence, and the result includes a high rate of masculine maladjustment and academic failure in the early school setting. Girls, on the other hand, continue to associate achievement with the need for approval and continue to achieve only if approval is forthcoming. In later years, where achievement is bought primarily as the result of autonomy, this early learning proves disadvantageous to them. In consequence, those women who go on to careers tend to be those who throughout childhood and adolescence have escaped the hegemony of traditional nurturant-domestic female sex role concerns. They have been influenced more by their fathers, or by the occasional and exceptional mastery-instigating teachers, than by their mothers.

While it is not surprising that autonomous and masterful competencies (more usually identified with male child-rearing) should be required for success in the larger social world, it is a surprise that we both wonder why women do not generally show so much of these competencies, and yet educate them so they cannot. They are expected to be less rebellious and to be more conforming in the school setting. Their political socialization involves a closer dependence on family and traditional points of view. They are significantly more affected by both family and school attitudes in almost every conceivable way than are the more unpredictable boys.

For those females who do achieve career status, there is continuing occupational pressure from males, nevertheless, to assume a mask of traditional female values. Those females are usually regarded as more successful who, while achieving on the one hand, are able to retain on the other the "mask of inferiority." As one of our female students expresses it, this mask includes the appearance of being happy, pleasant, and a little bit unorganized. Preferably the achiever does not show much obvious aggressiveness or participate in the usual masculine crudities. Any slight display of aggressiveness will earn her the title of a "castrating bitch." So great is the pressure from society in general, that most adolescent girls prefer to deemphasize their achievement rather than risk rejection from the opposite-sex peers whose approval they so desperately seek. Still, it is a part of the point being made here that these contents of the sex role are not necessarily irreversible, even if widespread. We might give as an example the quite potent "retraining" in sex role currently being exercised by women's liberation groups. These in some ways resemble initiation rites in which the incumbent, trained to a dependent role, must now be sufficiently severely treated so that a new and more independent role becomes possible. As in family therapy, however, these training effects can only take on lasting functional significance for the woman if she is able to incorporate change in her sex role conceptions into the family scheme. And, indeed, some young couples are, as a consequence, reshuffling the family chores in an increasingly egalitarian manner, while others seek to change the patterns of response and expectations towards their own and others' children in liberation nursery schools.

An example from our own research testifies to the way in which sex role contents do in fact change over the course of development, and so must be responsive to later influences. Employing the longitudinal data of the Institute of Human Development, University of California, Berkeley (Macfarlane, 1938), it has been possible to examine long term changes in sex-typical characteristics as a function of age. Boys and girls do show expected sex differences in dependency, aggression, autonomy, and so on, during the years of middle childhood, though not of the magnitude cultural (familial) stereotypes would lead one to believe. However, subsequent Q sort studies (Block, 1970) of these same subjects during junior high school, senior high school, and adulthood (thirty years of age) fail to yield consistency in such gender-specific behaviors (dependency, aggression) as were observed in middle and late childhood. Sex-appropriate behaviors demonstrated in middle childhood lose their persisting character in later development; that is, they presumably change as the major influences on sex role extend increasingly to one's peers and schoolmates and are less confined to the immediate family.

In conclusion, the major contribution of the sociologist to our understanding of sex role is in his shift from a basically biological model with a social superstructure, as is illustrated by the psychoanalytic model, to a social structural model residing implicitly on a biological base. Sex role development from this point of view provides a less restricted conception of man and places emphasis on those subtle relations of behavior to a social order that appears to be peculiar to man. The merit of the approach is its emphasis on the belief that sex role learning cannot be conceptualized as only instinct-directed or person-directed, but also involves the covert but significant interaction of man with the social structure in which his entire learning experience occurs. The family represents a configuration of social effects on the sex role, as surely as the fundamental sex of the child influences the nature of effects emerging from the parent and sibling.

It would be a difficult task to construct an articulate argument in disagreement with Parson's functionalist contention that the child-rearing processes are in some way bound to the larger functional patterns of society. Whether the behavior roles are divided between the sexes, and whether this division affects the children in quite the neat and systematic way that Parsons contends is another matter. One only has to read *Sexual Politics* by Kate Millet (1970) to be made aware of the assumptions about masculine superiority implicit in this theory as well as in earlier Freudian theory. However, although her critique may invalidate the inevitablity of the expressive-instrumental distinction between the sexes, it in no way questions the more general assumption that sex role development is included in larger social processes.

VII

The Language of
Anthropology

THE ANTHROPOLOGIST, like the sociologist, is concerned with the determining influence of the particular social pattern within which the subject is embedded, but adds to his study of each specific culture a knowledge of many different social patterns. He approaches not merely immediate social determination, but also more universal questions, and in doing so studies the role of different societies (the social patterns) and cultures (the systems of traditions) in human adaptation. Like the biologist he can propose certain conditions that are necessary for survival. This chapter will return to the question presented in Chapter 2 as to whether man is born with the genetic materials for sex role development or whether he is born plastic and is subsequently shaped into this role. However, the argument is carried on in this chapter through a comparison of typical and atypical cultures rather than through a comparison of typical and atypical animals or individual human beings. Much of the present chapter will rely on the work of Margaret Mead (1935, 1961, 1969), who is the most widely known exponent of this type of thinking in the area of sex role development.

In anthropology, the "givens" are the existing institutions, customs, and taboos which allow the society to cohere and continue. Much of the discussion in this chapter will have to do with the effects of such patterning on sex role development. Anthropologists are also concerned with adaptation and the way in which these patterns contribute to group survival; this will be our concern later in the chapter.

CULTURE AND SEX ROLE

The orientation of psychology is to define sex differences and sex role identification in terms of personal characteristics. In contrast, anthropology generally defines sex differences and sex role identification in terms of social and cultural processes. Thus, the differences between the sexes are not simply characteristics of the individual; they are culturally transmitted patterns of behavior determined in part by the functioning of society. Anthropologists emphasize that contrary to the expectations of those reared in our own culture, males and females differ in a variety of ways that are a consequence of cultural institutionalization, for example, social status, phantasy production, interpersonal behavior, gender identity, and so on.

Generally speaking, the anthropologist attempts to explain human behavior in terms of the acquisition of cultural directions and values, though there are some variations on this bias. Some anthropologists, for example, argue more modestly that the cultural setting exercises its influence upon behavior only in order to satisfy the instinctual demand. Nevertheless, as sex role behavior does vary from one society to another, the modifiability of the expression of any sex instinct through learning is indicated.

THE FAMILY SETTING

The anthropologist's view of sex role development, like that of the sociologist, emphasizes learning within the context of the nuclear and extended family. As a result, much effort has been made to examine the differences in household composition, sleeping arrangements, settlement patterns, and residence patterns, and their subtle relation to the environment and the economy of the society, since these factors appear to be central to the child-rearing practices that give rise to appropriate gender identity.

Most families in our society consist of a father, a mother, and unmarried sons and daughters (the nuclear family). This arrangement is far less universal than is generally believed. Murdock (1957) studied 565 societies and found that approximately one-quarter of them employed this pattern. Some three-quarters of the societies studied presented arrangements in which fathers sleep in clubs, in which extended families contain the married sons and daughters and their spouses, in which mothers and children live without the father, or in which the children are communally raised apart from their native parents. These discrepancies should result in remarkably different worlds for the children as well as in the employment of different socialization practices, as was indicated in a study by Whiting, Kluckhohn, and Anthony (1958), which made plain the great problems in cross-sex identification for a male in the societies in which the mother-child bond existed alongside the absence of the father. In the societies examined the boy spent all his early years with the mother to himself. The absence of the father as an identification model possessing power and control over resources appeared to create difficulty in appropriate adoption of gender role. As a consequence of the absence, the boy identified with the mother rather than with males. Whiting found that severe initiation rites involving painful hazing, trials of endurance, and genital operations prevailed in those societies in which fathers were physically or psychologically removed and the mother maintained an exclusive proximity to the child for the first years of life. These rites were maintained as necessary to counter father-rivalry, incest, and the tendency of the boy to identify with the mother. Though our own society lacks an institutionalized father-absence condition, Whiting demonstrated that these cross-cultural findings are replicated, in part, within our own society by showing that males who grew up close to their mothers and in the absence of fathers revealed similar aggressive protest against social rules. That is to say, he suggested that though our society does not have clearly institutionalized initiation rites to educate these boys in the requirements of the larger male society, one might interpret in a less formalized way the training which does take place, for example, in the prescriptions of delinquent gangs, military schools, and even in prisons (Harrington, 1970). Actually, this "evidence" is most tenuous, as the underlying assumption is that there is an equivalence among societies which do and those which do not institutionalize father-absence. Obviously, the reasons for father-absence in our culture are diverse, and more often than not associated with negative outcomes for *all* members of the family, not merely the young boy. Since this is the case, it is difficult to see this generalization as being coercive in nature, especially so since the "ritualizations" he mentions are generally punitive. While there is considerable argument among anthropologists as to whether the boy's psychosexual identification with the mother is what leads to the initiation rites in these societies, or whether the rites are there in the first place as a means of social communication, it is sufficient for our purposes that we recognize the dramatic effect that a particular family arrangement can have on sex role development.

THE FUNCTION OF ROLE ASSIGNMENT

Just as the character of the family can be shown to have an "arbitrary" effect on sex role, so can it be argued that sex role assignment works in equally arbitrary ways. There are few bases other than sex for social distinction among the newborn. Accordingly, Dornbusch (1966) suggests that one of the major reasons for sex differences in cultural prescription is that sex role assignment is the means whereby we justify not having to train each child in *every* type of activity. If society classifies all newborns into categories based on the probability that members of each category will engage in a specific set of adult behaviors, he says, then it is economical and to society's advantage to do so. As a result, training practices may emphasize the characteristics appropriate to the ascribed status, and minimize repetition among individuals. Since sex role is thus conceived as a status variable, once the identification of gender is made the society can begin anticipatory socialization in the early years. Illustrating an extreme anthropological position, Linton (1936) states:

> All societies prescribe different attitudes and activities to men and to women. Most of them try to rationalize these prescriptions in terms of the physiological difference between the sexes or their different roles in reproduction. While such factors may have served as a starting point for the development of a division, the actual ascriptions are almost entirely determined by culture [p. 18].

Once the ascriptive status occurs (i.e., the identification as a male or a female), what preparatory activities are entered upon for establishing the role identity? While in America there are two basic sex role stereotypes offered to children, in many societies there are more. For example, Mead (1961) enumerates eleven formal sex roles that are available in a variety of cultures. These include married females who bear children; married males who beget and provide for children; adult males who do not marry and beget children but who exercise some prescribed social function involving celibacy, sexual abstinence, and renunciation of procreation; adult males who assume female roles; adult females who assume male roles, including transvestitism; adult females (or, less frequently, males) who maintain themselves economically by the exploitation of sex relationships with extramarital partners; adults whose special, nonprocreative ceremonial role is important; adults of whom various forms of transvestitism and adoption of the behavior of the opposite sex are expected, so that the external genital morphology is either ignored or denied, for example, shamans (p. 1451). Any or all of these adult roles may occur in the same society, and there is the possibility of a child's choosing or being placed into one of these roles whenever the role is present and widely recognized. Thus, in some societies children are watched carefully and tested at early ages to determine what role they will fit best, that is, warrior, religious celibate, transvestite male, and so on. Elaborate prescriptions for correct social behavior are available, and once the choice is made, these are formally taught to the child. As Mead notes, "The cues used in different societies in assignment of any of these roles vary widely [p. 1452]." For example, bravery is a determining point among the Plains Indians, and thus a timid male child may be assigned the role of the transvestite. A child's preference for feminine occupation may provide the basis for role assignment, or, where female and male sex roles are differentiated in terms of their perception of softness and harshness of clothing, tactile sensitivity in a male child may be the first cue which leads his parents, his peers, or himself to assign him to the feminine role. Mead emphasizes that almost any item of human behavior may become involved in establishing a child's sex role. As an example of this diversity, those items on which our society depends as indicators of role assignment, especially gender-specific third-person pronouns and differentiation of names and clothing, may be completely absent in other societies. For example, she notes that there are many peoples where male and female names are not differentiated, and where there is no sex differentiation in the language! There are peoples where boys and girls are dressed exactly alike, a remarkable contrast to those cultures where children go without clothing so that the anatomic differences between the sexes are conspicuous since infancy. The failure to emphasize sex differences and sex-related behaviors is so pervasive that in some cultures of this order, although expressive and postural cues in behavior are characteristic of mature individuals of one sex or the other, these cues appear in all the young regardless of the sex of the child. For instance, where boys are classed with women until initiation, as in Iatmul (Bateson, 1958; Mead, 1949), a strong tendency toward female posture may be found in both preadolescent boys and girls. When girls are classed with men until bethrothal, as in Manus (Mead, 1956), a strong tendency toward male posture and behavior may be found in both boys and girls! Again, among the Arapesh, men and women are quite alike in their cooperativeness and concern for others, and passivity and unaggressiveness characterize both roles (Mead, 1961); that is, according to Western standards, both genders are equally feminine. In contrast, among the Tchambuli, aspects of what we consider to be the prevailingly masculine role, namely, dominance and the failure to reveal emotion, are uniformly characteristic of the female.

A further example is found in Spiro's (1956) description of Kibbutz life in Israel. Here, the emphasis is on equality of the genders, with no sexual division of labor. Women spend part of their time driving the tractors and toiling in the field, while men, on their part, help with the laundry and kitchen work. One might conclude that almost any cultural patterning that emphasizes sex similarities or differences appears workable.

LEARNING SEX ROLE

It is clear from these examples that sex role behavior, as well as all other roles in the culture, is patterned. It may be assumed that this common regulation assures minimum disruption. From this point of view, all behavior—sex role, adult role, maternal behavior, and so on—is ordered or regulated by the early translation through socialization of infantile impulses to anticipated role assignment. Mead (1961) employs the term "cognitive rehearsal" to describe this channelizing of human disposition into accepted forms of behavior appropriate to cultural preservation. The creation of this necessary and essential sex role identity requires that the adult show caution in the manner in which the infant is handled, that he allow the types of experiences appropriate to the child's sex, that the child learn the requisite interpersonal roles between sexes, that he understand his relation to others of different age and sex, and that he form a proper attitude toward his own body. In a psychologist's language, those attitudes, identities, and behaviors which are *preadaptive* of adult sex roles must be taught. Mead (1961) employs the term "prefigurative," and suggests:

> The child learns from slightly older children's openly expressed disapproval and disgust, as well as from the bitter, gossiping voice of his grandmother, how attitudes toward the body and sex relationships to other persons are patterned within that society. Each age learns from each other age. This child who is learning self-control and ways of meeting the requirements of modesty is constantly reminded by the immodesty and lack of self-control of a younger child [p. 1456].

The community or culture as a whole establishes patterns of behavior by employing what are essentially educational techniques, administering the reinforcement of approval and disapproval in accord with child's "rights" and "wrongs" which are based on his sex and age. In these circumstances, as Skinner (1953) notes, the adoption of a behavior leads to the support of a custom or manner, so that the maintenance of a sex-appropriate pattern in a sense becomes self-sustaining. One of the assumptions here is that the culture is an ongoing phenomenon, independent of any particular generation, so that institutionalized roles (e.g., sex role) must be filled in order for the system to continue. Most adult members of the culture, in addition to the parent, serve as socializing agents for the child. An example of this multiplicity of teachers is clear in the Nyansongo (Kenya), studied by LeVine and LeVine (1963), where any adult of the tribe will act to punish or discourage the expressions of aggression and sexuality that are frowned upon by the society at large. Rewards are typically verbal, while punishments are both verbal and physical; all responses are used to inculcate socially valued characteristics in the child.

In sum, the acquisition of behaviors linked with sex role characteristics and development is said to be dependent upon the parameters of the society in which the child finds himself, and the functional relationship of those behaviors to the basic requirements, the "musts" that the society satisfies in order to continue. Human sex role development can be, for example, the means of implementing a particular society's requirement for additional or fewer births. Females may be reared to be sexually receptive but not too receptive, and males may be reared to be sexually active, but to a limited degree. The societies' definition and differentiation of gender roles is intertwined with these necessities. We find this in societies which permit varying types of sexual activity at different ages, as in requiring chastity in unmarried girls and granting great sexual freedom to a married woman (Metraux & Mead, 1954), or in permitting homosexual relations among young males prior to marriage but allowing only heterosexual relations after marriage (Wirz, 1922).

For the anthropologist, then, all humans experience extreme dependency on adults, and have prolongation of maturation. The culture in which they live provides different mechanics creating what appear to be crucial alterations in the life state and physical makeup of the individuals. This results in uniformity across cultures for some male and female behaviors, and remarkable distinctions in other activities. All behaviors operate to sustain societal function, minimize conflict, maximize reproductive activity, safeguard family life, facilitate food gathering, and so on.

SEX ROLE FUNCTIONALISM

To this point we have emphasized the relativity of sex role to cultural patterns. Margaret Mead's writings have treated both this relativity and the virtue of cultural differences as symbolized by the United Nations.

However, recently among other anthropologists there has been a reconsideration of those elements which mankind has in common, and the cross-cultural studies have contributed to this review. For example, after examining data from 110 cultures, Barry, Bacon, and Child (1957) concluded that most cultures pressure toward the development of nurturance, obedience, and responsibility in girls, and toward self-reliance, independence, and achievement in boys. Further, D'Andrade (1966) pointed out that most societies are organized around males rather than females, and the natural accompaniment of this arrangement is a predictable assignment of duties, rights, and social status defining male and female sex roles. He notes the frequency with which cultures endow men with authority in legal and moral matters, yielding predictably greater power and authority to the male with a consequently greater value or prestige placed on the masculine role. In fact, this pattern is so widespread, he indicates, that there are few societies in which deferent behavior for men is prescribed.

While some have interpreted these nearly universal differences between the sexes as confirmation of culturally instigated behaviors, to most observers they seem to indicate that there must be some substantial biological impetus toward such role differences. From this point of view, the various atypical examples given earlier only show that human nature is malleable, but not that physiological differences between the sexes are not important. They must be important, it is argued, because most cultures have preferred to take physiological variations into account and elaborate on them rather than ignore them as in the atypical examples given. The evidence certainly suggests that all known human societies acknowledge the anatomical and functional differences between males and females, even if in subtle and complex ways. This recognition may be revealed in the nuances in behavior, posture, stance, and gait of the individual, or may be overtly indicated in the language, ornamentation, dress, division of labor, legal status, religious role, and so on.

All known human populations yield males and females who differ in primary sex characteristics, and in many secondary sex characteristics. Males typically are of greater height, strength, and hairiness, and possess a higher muscle-to-fat ratio, more massive skeleton, and so on. This poses the question regarding the extent to which anatomic-structural differences in the sexes restrict the range of possible behaviors that the child may be taught. In short, to what extent is there a natural, intrinsic relation between the physiological sex of the individual and the realm of behaviors which may be patterned? For the comparative psychologist (Ch. 2), who sees structural and genetic factors as directly related to sex-correlated activities, it is a logical step to argue that man, like lower animals, comes equipped with dispositions and physical characteristics that dictate the kinds of behaviors which emerge as sex-appropriate. For example, since males are typically larger and have a higher muscle-to-fat ratio, it seems to the psychologist only sensible to make the causal link between male physical makeup and the fact that in the division of labor in the majority of societies men are responsible for the activities that are more strenuous, cooperative, and that may require long periods of travel. D'Andrade (1966) presents an argument suggesting that this may be too simple a notion to account for the relationship between sex and behavior. He argues cogently that:

> . . . The division of labor by sex comes about as a result of generalization from activities directly related to physical sex differences to activities only indirectly related to these differences; that is, from behaviors which are differentially reinforced as a result of physical differences to behaviors which are anticipatory or similar to such directly conditioned activities [p. 178].

What he is suggesting is that there are physical differences which lead to specific activities and behaviors which may be considered preadaptive of the types of activities that are subsequently seen as sex-related behaviors.

It is clear that from an anthropological point of view, genetically determined constitutional types are insufficient to explain the acquisition and development of sex role. Thus, in the classical division of labor where males are more strenuous and mobile while females tend, in contrast, to be less strenuous and mobile, one might conclude not only that anatomic-structural differences render certain activities *more likely* by sex, but also that they lead to the reinforcement by sex of activities that are only indirectly related to physical makeup. But, as we have shown, this likelihood does not preclude the sharing or even the reversal in some cultures of what are considered to be stereotypically sex-appropriate behaviors.

At this point, one may argue "conservatively" that since most cultures have chosen to take the basic physiological sex differences into account, then it is wise to continue to do so. Alternatively, one may argue more "liberally" (because these differences are as much a matter of politics as they are of science) that given changing historical circumstances, man's early evolution is not a guide to the future. Let us assume for a moment a position which asserts that *control over the environment* (whether it be physical, social, or symbolic) is the sustaining force behind all role development, and particularly sex role development. In the most primitive setting, man's apparent lack of control over elemental forces leads to biological determinacy. That is, as in most of the animal kingdom, simple basic needs (birth, hunger) predominate, and such fundamental differentiators of males and females as size, muscle-fat ratio, and reactivity are directly related to need satisfaction and role development. Only those need systems sufficient for the preservation of self and small groups are evident, and role differentiation is simple; that is, males are warriors and foragers, females are housekeepers and childbearers. There is a direct and intrinsic relation between societal functions, role systems, and their implementation. The more primitive system, with its minimal control over the environment, requires fewer roles to sustain the system and relies on direct relations between biological makeup and role assignment. Biologically based sex differences (e.g., strength-weakness, mobility-fixity) are the principal determiners of role assignment. With decreasing primitivization and increasing control over the environment, cultural role development grows more complex as population and resource requirements increase. As these cultural roles evolve, sex-linked characteristics become less dependent on the original biological relations; in order to serve increasingly complex need systems, an extension or elaboration of functions occurs. As a result, man's strength and mobility, formerly important for life-sustaining functions, lose their saliency for defenses no longer required and are increasingly differentiated by training for qualities appropriate to more diverse functions, for example, strategic, entrepreneurial, magical, and so on. In turn, female housekeeping functions may be elaborated through training in nurturance, succorance, and dependency. Thus, as a society increases in complexity, the relations of role to morphology are less obvious. At this level of development, most sexually dimorphic behaviors are only indirectly related to the original biological role functions, and the sexes are increasingly capable of sharing in the trained-for activities. Socialization at this point involves training for far more complex, overlapping adult functions which produce a greater number of roles and ones that are less subject to restriction to one gender. In contemporary society, the process has been taken even further since control over the environment, as a result of dramatic technological innovations, has reached the maximal level. This fact strongly overrides whatever contingencies in the biological sense earlier dictated the assignation of behaviors to one sex or the other. Because there are more role functions to be served, both sexes are less restricted. Either sex can well serve most contemporary role requirements. Thus, the present status of what we have been calling environmental control, with only a few exceptions, eliminates the necessity for any clear separation of sex role functions.

It would be foolhardy, however, to conclude from this brief, inexact historical exegesis that males and females do not differ in what they bring to a situation and how they subsequently behave. Our interpretation argues only that psychological masculinity and femininity (gender roles) are far more complex and overlapping and are less distinguishable from one another than has been the case in earlier generations.

In sum, from this point of view we can declare that those who emphasize innate sex differences are either too interested in the literature on animals or too preoccupied with the earlier stages in man's evolution. In general, those who look toward the animal literature tend to over-emphasize birth differences and those who look toward the anthropological literature tend to underemphasize them. Perhaps we may illustrate the problem by saying that if an animal's ratio of heredity to environment is 1:1, in human beings the ratio is probably close to 1:10. Given this degree of flexibility in man, it is hard not to believe that the form of his sex role development will depend on whether contemporary culture wishes to underemphasize the differences between genders or to overplay them.

VIII

Resolution

IN THE ANTHROPOLOGICAL and the biological chapters, the central issue became the relative influence of the two types of determinants associated with these branches of knowledge. In the present chapter, this discussion is carried further, a sketch of a developmental resolution is provided, and finally, we will resume our introductory question of whether sex differences really matter.

BIOLOGY VS. ANTHROPOLOGY

When an issue is as long-standing as this one, it is unlikely to be terminated easily. What happens more often is that the questions and answers come to be treated in a more complex way than was originally the case. We summarized the material on animal and human biology by suggesting that sex differences have been clearly established at birth, so that one cannot legitimately speak of the human organism as psychosexually *neutral*. Yet, the clinical materials on children reared in a sex role different from that suggested by their physical endowment showed clearly that these birth differences *can* be ignored without devastating consequences. The anthropological materials on the diverse forms of sex role learning in different cultures heightened this clinical picture. There are cultures where, given our Western conception of sex roles, men are like women and women are like men. Therefore, it was possible to derive a picture of sex role relativism from both the clinical and anthropological literature. Regardless of biological sex differences at birth, there are cases in our own culture as well as other entire cultures where what we think of as "traditional" sex differences are ignored, apparently without adverse effects. And yet it is equally clear that within our own culture, most individuals

79

are reared in the sex toward which they are disposed by their physical endowment, and that cross-culturally, males and females tend to differ in a fairly universal manner. We conclude from this that despite the malleability of the infant organism, most cultures have chosen to satisfy their basic functions by capitalizing on these differences at birth rather than by ignoring them. They have then gone on to use the sex dichotomy as one of the most economical ways of managing cultural functions. The contemporary question thus becomes: is it ultimately more efficient for human adaptation if we continue to notice these birth differences than if we choose to ignore them?

We do think it necessary at this point, having arrived at a level of generalization where we place the greatest weight on cultural variables rather than on biological ones, to add the precaution that, as psychologists, we are liable to overemphasize psychological and cultural explanations and underemphasize biological ones. The obvious difficulty in approximating the relationship between genetics and behavior with any degree of precision may well tempt us to assign a socio-psychological cause to those kinds of behavior where there is as yet no way of ascertaining the extent to which a genetic base is relevant.

DEVELOPMENTAL TRANSFORMATIONS

The view has been taken that in humans, *nurture* can ignore *nature,* but usually chooses not to do so. In this way the assertions of anthropologists and biologists are grandly reconciled. The variant claims of psychoanalysts, social learning theorists, and so on, are not so easily adjusted. Our own preference (as in our earlier book, *The Sibling*) is for a reconciliation in which it is shown that *each theory is particularly appropriate to certain types of data at certain age levels.* Psychoanalysis seems to tell us best about the origins of the affective aspects of sex role development in infancy; social learning theory does its best work in accounting for modeling behavior in childhood; sociology demonstrates the cognitive linkage of these sex roles to broader adult familial and occupational roles; and anthropology is able to illustrate the way in which sex role, particularly in adolescence, is one of the distinctive forms of cultural functioning.

Obviously, only an extended account would be sufficient to fully state and justify an approach of this sort. In this conclusion we can sketch only some of the questions and issues that we consider to be important.

The first question that arises is whether the principal cause of the behavioral differences between the sexes is the early discrepancies in treatment, the differences in treatment throughout the individual's life, or those in later life. By and large, psychoanalytic and social learning theory have been perceived as favoring explanations which emphasize early treatment differences, and sociology and anthropology as favoring explanations which focus on the variations in continuous treatment. Thus, an emphasis on the formative character of the mother-child relationship or on the importance of early reinforcements tends to be linked with the view that sex role differences are established during infancy. For evidence supportive of this theory one can cite the contrasting ways in which mothers do treat boy and girl babies, or Money's (1963) clinical data justifying his claim that the basics of sex identity are acquired by the age of three years. Contrary to this view, one can cite the fact that the bulk of the mother's behavior to babies of both sexes is the same, namely, taking care of and nurturing the child. While in the past classic learning approaches apparently implied that primary and unsymbolized learnings were most important, modern statements of the theory clearly do not place so much weight on this early learning: behavior that does not continue to be reinforced is expected to extinguish. Therefore, if sex role development is an outcome of behavior shaping, then behavior must be continually shaped and reinforced throughout subsequent years if it is to persist. Similarly, recent emphasis on modeling behaviors that call attention to the child's capacity for observational learning also implicitly affirm the importance of the later years of childhood. As we observe productively only that which we understand, and as understanding is relatively long in maturing, reaching formal abstract levels only in adolescence, it follows that much of sex role development must rest on later modeling capacities. Consequently, there is currently no reason to believe that social learning theories imply "infant determinism," although that position was once generally maintained (Orlansky, 1949). Perhaps here we need to distinguish between sex-role typing or labeling which does appear to occur early (Money, 1963) and the contents of this basic categorization which may change throughout a lifetime. The early categorizing does seem to be determining of whether one perceives oneself as boy or girl. What that means, however, can take a lifetime to decide.

While psychoanalysis places great weight in development as a whole on the mother-child relationship, the focus in sex role learning, as we have seen, is on the events of the Oedipal crisis which occurs during the period from four to six years. In sociology and anthropology, at the other extreme, since the infant or child socialization arrangements are only mediators of sex role functions in the adult culture, adult discriminations and decisions have primary importance. We can see that none of the theories presented here places sole responsibility for sex role development on the events in the early mother-child relationship.

If the infant's early years are not seen as of *decisive* importance, the question arises as to what is important about those years? Here, both social learning and psychoanalysis have implied that the quality of the mother's nurturing or dependency relationship is primary because it becomes the basis for her effectiveness later as a shaper of the child's behavior. Because of his dependency on the mother, the child in due course adopts her values. What she wants, the child becomes. Recently, however, Kohlberg (1969) has criticized this view and in effect reversed the definition of what is important in early childhood. He says that the important factor in sex role determination is *not* the child's relationship to the mother, but the child's own understanding:

> The child's basic sex role identity is largely the result of self-categorization as a male or female made early in development. While dependent upon social labelling, this categorization is basically a cognitive reality judgment rather than a product of social rewards, parental identifications, or sexual fantasies [p. 431].

In fact, having made the categorization, the child subsequently becomes interested in those things that members of his sex prefer, and identifies with other members of his own sex for sex role purposes. This is the reverse of the social learning point of view which states that the child is initially dependent on others and consequently becomes a boy or girl in order to obtain the rewards they offer. Instead, Kohlberg assumes that the child, exercising his competence in terms of his own self-categorization, reaches out for those phenomena and values he finds relevant. Kohlberg's major piece of evidence underlying this argument is that mental age predicts more of the variance in any measure of sex role development than other measures such as parental nurturance, similarity to the parent of the same sex, and so on.

While Kohlberg's thesis is a useful antidote to social learning, it also has its oversimplifications. The contrast between the views has arisen in part because of the traditional neglect in social learning and psychoanalytic theory of cognitive factors as guiding agencies. What tends to be neglected by Kohlberg, however, is evidence indicating that the child's very self and other categorizations are themselves facilitated by the quality of his relationship to the mother. We can see that there is an intimate interaction between affective and cognitive variables throughout the child's development, and the real problem is to elucidate the subtleties of this interaction rather than to posit that either affective or cognitive variables are more basic. It might also be argued that just as social learning theory tends to overemphasize the passivity of the organism under parental treatment, Kohlberg's approach (called cognitive-developmental theory) tends to overemphasize the autonomous role of the active organism in its own self-determination. Social learning and cognitive-development theories complement one another, and there is a long philosophical tradition behind their respective viewpoints (Langer, 1969). In our judgment, each has only partial relevance, its usefulness dependent on which variables are being discussed and on which parent-child relationships are being considered. Social learning theory speaks with more relevance to affective variables, and cognitive-developmental theory with more relevance to cognitive variables. There are authoritarian parents who overdetermine most aspects of the child's behavior; and there are parents whose controls are relaxed, so that the children are self-determining in most matters. The balance between parent and child is a factor in deciding the relevance of each theory in the individual case.

Another issue of importance for the early childhood years is whether the establishment of sex role identity is a smooth or a discordant process. According to Freudian psychology, sex role identity is based on conflict and defense. In the other theories the processes indicated are less conflicting. While this must again be partly a matter of individual differences, cross-cultural evidence does seem to suggest that all forms of socialization have become increasingly troublesome with the development of greater cultural complexity. It is possible that the modern trend toward decreasing the severity of sex role socialization occurs because it is being made subordinate to the more important rigors of raising a child to function from an early age in this symbolically complex culture.

Whatever their specific views concerning the earliest years, all these theories consider that important developments occur in the transition from early to middle childhood, the fourth through the eighth year. In fact, sex role identification is one of the major criteria for this development. We need not argue whether the shift is better explained in terms of the realignments of parental attachments (psychoanalysis), the modeling of parents and peers of the same sex (social learning), the cognitive capacity to make a more consistent categorization (cognitive-developmental), or the grouping of sex division for functional work (cultural requirements), but we can hope that in future research there may be less emphasis on demonstrating the potency of only one of these contenders and more emphasis on devising research designs to illustrate the interaction and relative contribution of all these theories (Bandura, Ross, & Ross, 1963; Heilbrun, 1965; Mussen & Distler, 1959).

With our emphasis on the relevance of theories of sex role development for particular stages in development, it should be made clear that some periods of development have not yet received sufficient theoretical or empirical attention. The early, formative years (through, let us say, the seventh year of life) have been intensively studied for decades. The reasons for this are several, including the drama of change so clearly depicted here, the availability of the subjects, and certainly, the overriding importance heretofore given to the notion of infant-determinism. A relatively neglected area is preadolescence, though admittedly it is a period of considerable change in sex role development (Sutton-Smith, Rosenberg, & Morgan, 1963). With a few exceptions (Sullivan, 1947; Parsons, 1964), it has not recently received the theoretical attention it deserves. Instead, the older literature on this period is replete with popular (applied?) concepts with little theoretical breadth, for example, the "negativism" of eleven-year-old girls (Frank, 1953), and somewhat more interesting, the data concerning the effect on boys and girls of early and late maturation during this period (Jersild, 1963). The onset of the pubertal growth spurt, the capacity for abstract categorization, the increased influence of peers as models, and the differentiation between peer group and adult authority are obviously important considerations which should all be taken into account in any adequate theoretical framework.

With adolescence, the issue sharpens as to whether sex role development is a limited occurrence or a continuous series of events. Despite the obvious crucial importance of this period for sex role behavior, given the profound physiological and psychological changes involved, the research as well as theoretical literature is remarkably lacking. Erikson (1950), varying from traditional psychoanalysis, posits that sex role identity involves a series of developmental crises or changes in self-concept. He contends that sex role identity is not completed by the end of middle childhood, but undergoes changes in the course of adolescent and early adult experience. This notion differs markedly from traditional Freudian ideas which, as we have seen, cite the resolution of the Oedipal situation as the basis for the sudden and complete development of sex role identification. Erikson's implication that masculinity-femininity is, in some sense, continuous as a personality variable is probably to some extent true. That is to say, the quality and significance of sex role behavior and its relation to the total personality may well change as a function of age. For example, high masculinity may have great reward value in adolescence, reducing the development of other coping behaviors, and causing minimal "payoff" in early adulthood, where masculinity alone is insufficient. The highly masculine adolescent boy whose size, coordination, and outgoingness are at a premium may be very popular, good at athletics, and a central figure in most activities during this period. Contrarily, the adolescent boy low on masculinity may have adjustment problems (Mussen, 1962) such as unpopularity, detachment, and a sense of being inferior. The nonreinforcing conditions in the latter case may well activate already existing compensatory dispositions (e.g., intellectualism, aesthetic appreciation, concern with social problems) whose "payoff" value is low in adolescence but very high in adulthood. Mussen (1961) found, in fact, that a high degree of masculinity in adolescence was generally associated with concurrent emotional security, masculine boys possessing a more positive self-concept and showing greater self-confidence overall. However, these same boys, as adults, were described as lacking adjustment and marginally adequate in most social behaviors. Mussen (1962) concludes that "certain adolescent instrumental characteristics of the highly masculine subjects decreased after adolescence, while correlatively, the less masculine group changed in a favorable direction [p. 439]." One conclusion may be that the prestige value of high masculinity in adolescence may inhibit the development of those attributes particularly relevant to success in social and vocational pursuits in adulthood. It is noteworthy that socioeconomic class level limits the generality of this formulation, since the likelihood is great that in lower socioeconomic groupings high masculinity continues to have great reward value as long as one remains confined to this specific social grouping. This data suggests that the very nature of sex role achievement is directly related to one's developmental stage, and its qualities and mode of expression are contingent on age-peer group emphases. In addition, the lack of adjustment found with less adequate sex role behavior may sometimes lead to the development of coping activities that would remain latent or underdeveloped in the absence of stress.

In this developmental account of certain approaches, in which we have cited their partiality as well as their partial appropriateness in accounting for some variables at some age levels, there is implicit the assumption that it may be possible to develop an "interactional terminology" to encompass all these different areas of study. At this time, we will suggest the outlines for such an interactional terminology.

The different theories of sex and identity have been seen to place ultimate determination either within the biological system or within the cultural system. The two chapters on psychoanalysis and social learning might be considered accounts of theories that attempt to deal with interactions between the two sets of limits, with psychoanalysis more disposed to biological explanation and social learning to cultural explanation. Both are, in this sense, "mediating" theories.

A recent contender for this central "interactionist" position is the cognitive-developmental theory as presented by Kohlberg (1969). Kohlberg views cognitive structure as the result of processes of interaction between biology and culture, and therefore as the central focus for an interactional theory. Unfortunately, he does not define the way in which the biological and sociological structures are assimilated into his key cognitive interrelationships. He implies, in fact, that sociological explanations in terms of family, peer group, or social class structures are largely fruitless. What is important is not the institutional form of these entities, but the opportunity they provide for the cognitive process of role taking. It is this role taking, alone, which gives the subject insight into alternative viewpoints, so that his own cognitive structures are influenced, and in that way his own self-categorization as boy or girl is further differentiated. Kohlberg argues that there are various stages in the development of role-taking opportunities, and that different groups are probably, at distinct times, well-suited in their requirements to the cognitive level of the child. This is an interesting notion, but awaits further research for meaning in the study of individual growth.

Even Kohlberg's own data, however, indicates that subjects in the earlier and more concrete stages of this developmental system are more influenced by situational factors than are subjects in his higher stages of cognitive development. It would seem that only with the advent, near age eleven, of what Piaget has termed "formal operations" (an internalized, "abstract" rule system) that cognitive structures have an independent influence on sex role choice and development. While the child's own conceptualizations and self-identifications must play some mediating role in the earlier years, at this time we lack sufficient evidence to argue that these factors are any more important in early childhood than are the social learning effects of parents and others.

However, the question has been recognized; namely, how do we take the biological constituents and the cultural constituents and develop a psychological theory that will adequately account for the emerging sex and identity of the given individual? Kohlberg's effort, with its emphasis on the organism's role in this process, is certainly novel when compared with the decades of emphasis on the overpowering influence of parental actions (both in psychoanalysis and derivatives of social learning theory). Yet, as we have seen, his theory perhaps too readily slights these traditional approaches in areas where it would be more helpful to subsume them into some broader point of view.

The first problem confronted by the interactional structure, as the previous review of theories has suggested, is to discover how genetic (chromosomal) and maturational (hormonal) factors enter into the determination of gender. Following this we must determine how these bio-logical variables interact with the various forms of behavior evocation and modification discussed by social learning theorists. The next question is how the cultural system leads to the presentation in a patterned manner of the behavioral influences on the child. Finally, we must consider how ego-psychological factors (identification, cognition, self-concept, etc.) are de-termined by, mediate, or determine the impact and interaction of these other factors. While sex, as we have used the term throughout the book, is defined by only the biological variables of the first category above, identity is a more comprehensive construct and has been used in this work as a summative term for all the influences mentioned. One's sex role identity is an outcome of all the influences: biological, psychological, and cultural.

There is one aspect of sex role identity that has been neglected in this work, namely, the sex role self-concept. The phenomenological sense of one's own sex role identity is obviously very important in determining behavior and yet has been little studied, partly because it has usually been included in the general derogation of cognitive factors, assumed to be an epiphenomenon of other influences, not itself in any way of importance in psychological studies. While this position may have some justification when one is speaking of young children with little self-awareness, whose behavior is largely under the control of individual impulses and social or environmental forces, the position becomes increasingly irrelevant as the child's personal awareness plays a more significant role in his behavior. In adolescence, for example, self-assessment devices sometimes reveal key information quite at variance with what might have been supposed using more customary predictors of sex role status. Conventional predictors (physique, social status) may be negated by other predictors (sibling status) in a way that is realizable only through knowledge of the subject's personal assessment. For example, a young boy may possess physique and coordination which would normally be associated with high masculinity in adolescence. But if he has three sisters, his family configuration may dispose to introspective, intuitive behavior—quite opposed to morpho-logic expectations. Jones (1943) gives the example of an athletic and scholarly boy much sought after by members of the other sex, who as a younger brother, was nevertheless preoccupied with persisting feelings of inferiority. There is another example from the Berkeley longitudinal data of a group of early maturing girls who, though unpopular with their classmates and teachers, felt satisfied with their sex role status, apparently because of their immediate appreciation of their own physical develop-ment.

Even more important is the evidence that most individuals can learn to behave in a manner appropriate to their sex role without giving any indication as to how they feel about it. There can be a chronic disparity between how one sees himself as a man or a woman and how one has been conditioned to respond in the presence of others. After all, many aspects of self (especially the sexual self) have been continuously reinforced since early childhood so that appropriate responses in most instances are rather automatic, that is, one learns to respond to the obvious in a manner expected of him by others. As a result, overt behavior may be less than revealing.

These examples will indicate that the term *identity* as used in this work refers to a complex outcome of many levels of operation (psychodynamic impulses, habits, status, cognitions, self-consciousness, self-awareness) undoubtedly knit together in some patterned system from the biological and sociological forces. No investigation to date has searched for an explanation in such multidimensional terms as we suggest here; therefore, we cannot speak more precisely of the patterns themselves. We would emphasize, however, that regardless of early determination, eventually sex role identity becomes inseparable from the larger identity in terms of which the individual conceptualizes his own existence.

DO SEX DIFFERENCES REALLY MATTER?

It would be difficult to read the materials of the previous chapters without deriving the feeling that sex differences certainly have mattered in most human cultures throughout history and that they still matter to the biologists, psychologists, and sociologists who study them. But perhaps all this is, as we suggested in the introduction, merely "conservatism." We have also shown that although there are biological differences between the sexes at birth, the overlap in behavior between the sexes is so extensive and human malleability so great that both sexes are capable of exhibiting most forms of human behavior. At this time there are few behaviors that may be viewed as solely within the province of one sex. The fact that human cultures throughout history have made use of sex differences need not imply that they will continue to do so. It is possible, certainly, that the present authors' categorization of sex role differences as a convenient but typological error is, itself, an expression of a culture pattern about to move in a direction emphasizing human and personality differences rather than gender-related discrepancies. If a more complex and a more creative culture requires the most extensive application of ability, it may no longer be able to afford status stereotypes that confine many intelligent members of one of the sexes to menial roles. The most important areas of change

are childbirth and child rearing, which no longer seem to be the irrevoca-
ble barrier they once were to the removal of sex role stereotypes. Giving
birth to a child hinders the female's mobility less than was traditionally
true, and women typically live for a longer period beyond the childbearing
and child-rearing years. It is commonplace to see a professional woman
take a brief period from her vocational pursuits in order to give birth to a
child, and the subsequent childcare becomes a shared activity of the
babysitter, nursery school, and both parents, with early resumption of the
woman's previous activity. The emphasis of the women's liberation move-
ment on free abortions and universal childcare arrangements clearly spells
out a recognition of the criticality of this long-time barrier to change. In
that case, the humanistic notion expressed above, that individual differences are more important than sex stereotypes, becomes itself merely a
vehicle for cultural changes of an even more radical sort. It seems reasonable to the humanist that some women would prefer motherhood and that
some would not, that some would prefer to care for their children themselves and that some would not, and that current changes would contribute
to great diversity and greater happiness. However, if in the insistence upon
equality we are disregarding many of the former special characteristics of
womanhood, then indeed, it will be demography and not diversity that is
being served.

What are the possible consequences for individuals in a society in
which sex differences are diminishing? Certainly, one possibility is a decrease in the problems surrounding the attainment of sex role identity, or
the self-perception of sex role adequacy.

What we have been saying may have some relevance for today's
youth with their increasing propensity to dress alike, to act alike, and to
treat one another warmly. Young persons appear bent on experience and
meanings which many parents are apparently incapable of sharing or
understanding. In a way, they are rebelling against the passive acceptance
of culturally transmitted values and behavior, including sex role values, as
though only through such rebellion can they free themselves from the
restrictions and hindrances in life which interfere with the search for
meaning. As the status differences (both sexual and economic) become less
crucial in dictating feelings and behaviors, presumably the relevance and
meaning in life become more accessible. There is a collective search for a
personal identity and meaning that can be shared. Distler (1968) has
suggested that males and females are becoming more expressive than
instrumental in their orientation (Parsons, 1964, Ch. 6). That is, both
sexes now focus on experiencing and finding meaning through the experiencing, rather than on attaining goals and relying on rationality as a way

of knowing, which has been a predilection of their elders. With this orientation, as we have suggested, they can eliminate many of the anxieties about their sex role, which in itself is changing, that appear to have been so much a part of traditional socialization practices.

Still, this is an optimistic view, and one that comes easily to professionals whose lives readily permit a reduction in the importance of sex differences. As we have emphasized throughout, history teaches another lesson. Most cultures have preferred to maximize sex differences rather than reduce them. It could be, therefore, that though some of today's sex differences may disappear, others may arise, for men and women may well invent new techniques for polarization. Our present typology may not be simply a psychometric error or a cultural habit. It may be that a society without sex stereotypes is much less interesting and productive than societies with definitions of sex role behavior.

REFERENCES

Aberle, D. F., & Naegele, K. D.   Middle class fathers' occupational role and attitudes toward children. *American Journal of Orthopsychiatry,* 1952, **22,** 366–378.

Aronson, L. R.   Environmental stimuli altering the physiological condition of the individual among lower vertebrates. In F. A. Beach (Ed.), *Sex and behavior.* New York: John Wiley & Sons, 1965. Pp. 290–318.

Baker, H. J., & Stoller, R. J.   Biological force postulated as having role in gender identity. *Roche Reports: Frontiers of Hospital Psychiatry,* 1967, **4,** 3.

Baldwin, A. L.   *Theories of child development.* New York: John Wiley & Sons, 1967.

Bales, R. F.   *Interaction process analysis, a method for the study of small groups.* Cambridge, Mass.: Addison-Wesley Press, 1950.

Bandura, A., Ross, D., & Ross, S.   Transmission of aggression through imitation of aggressive models. *Journal of Abnormal and Social Psychology,* 1961, **63,** 575–582.

Bandura, A., Ross, D., & Ross, S.   A comparative test of the status envy, social power, and secondary reinforcement theories of identificatory learning. *Journal of Abnormal and Social Psychology,* 1963, **67,** 527–534.

Bandura, A., & Walters, R. H.   *Social learning and personality development.* New York: Holt, Rinehart & Winston, 1963.

Barr, M. L., & Bertram, E. G.   A morphological distinction between neurons of the male and female, and the behavior of the nucleolar satellite during accelerated nucleoprotein synthesis. *Nature,* 1949, **163,** 676–677.

Barr, M. L., & Carr, D. H.   Sex chromatin, sex chromosomes and sex anomalies. *Canadian Medical Association Journal,* 1960, **83,** 979–986.

Barry, H., Bacon, M., & Child, I. L.   A cross-cultural survey of some sex differences in socialization. *Journal of Abnormal and Social Psychology,* 1957, **55,** 327–332.

Bateson, G.   *Naven.* (2nd ed.) Stanford, Calif.: Stanford University Press, 1958.

Beach, F. A.   Evolutionary changes in the physiological control of mating behavior in mammals. *Psychological Review,* 1947, **54,** 279–315.

Beach, F. A.   Neural and chemical regulation of behavior. In H. F. Harlow & C. N. Woolsey (Eds.), *Biological and biochemical bases of behavior.* Madison: University of Wisconsin Press, 1958. Pp. 263–284.

Beach, F. A. (Ed.)   *Sex and behavior.* New York: John Wiley & Sons, 1965.

Bell, R. Q.   Some factors to be controlled in studies of behavior of newborns. *Biologia Neonatorum,* 1963, **5,** 200–214.

93

Bell, R. Q., & Costello, N. S.   Three tests for sex differences in tactile sensitivity in the newborn. *Biologia Neonatorum,* 1964, **7,** 335–347.

Block, J.   *Lives through time.* Berkeley, Calif.: Bancroft Books, 1972.

Bremer, J.   *Asexualization, a follow up study of 244 cases.* New York: Macmillan, 1959.

Brim, O. J.   The parent-child relation as a social system: I. Parent and child roles. *Child Development,* 1957, **28,** 343–364.

Brim, O. J.   Family structure and sex role learning in children: A further analysis of Helen Koch's data. *Sociometry,* 1958, **21,** 1–16.

Brim, O. J.   Personality development as role learning. In I. Iscoe & H. Stevenson (Eds.), *Personality development in children.* Austin: University of Texas Press, 1960. Pp. 127–159.

Bronfenbrenner, U.   Freudian theories of identification and their derivatives. *Child Development,* 1960, **31,** 15–40.

Broverman, D. M., Klaiber, E. L., Kobayashi, Y., & Vogel, W.   Roles of activation and inhibition in sex differences in cognitive abilities. *Psychological Review,* 1968, **75,** 23–50.

Burns, R. K.   Role of hormones in the differentiation of sex. In W. C. Young (Ed.), *Sex and internal secretions.* Baltimore: Williams & Wilkins, 1961. Pp. 76–160.

Caspari, E. W.   The evolutionary importance of sexual processes and of sexual behavior. In F. A. Beach (Ed.), *Sex and behavior.* New York: John Wiley & Sons, 1965. Pp. 34–52.

Chang, C. Y., & Witschi, E.   Breeding of sex-reversed males of *Xenopus laevis daudin. Proceedings of the Society of Experimental Biology and Medicine,* 1956, **89,** 150–152.

Cottrell, L. S.   The adjustment of the individual to his age and sex roles. *American Sociological Review,* 1942, **7,** 617–620.

D'Andrade, R. G.   Sex differences and cultural institutions. In E. E. Maccoby (Ed.), *The development of sex differences.* Stanford, Calif.: Stanford University Press, 1966. Pp. 173–204.

DeVore, I.   Male dominance and mating behavior in baboons. In F. A. Beach (Ed.), *Sex and behavior.* New York: John Wiley & Sons, 1965. Pp. 266–289.

Diamond, M.   A critical evaluation of the ontogeny of human sexual behavior. *Quarterly Review of Biology,* 1965, **40,** 147–175.

Distler, L. S.   The adolescent "hippie" and the emergence of a matristic culture. Paper read at American Psychological Association meetings, San Francisco, August 1968.

Dollard, J., & Miller, N. E.   *Personality and psychotherapy: An analysis in terms of learning, thinking and culture.* New York: McGraw-Hill, 1950.

Dornbusch, S. M.   Afterword. In E. E. Maccoby (Ed.), *The development of sex differences.* Stanford, Calif.: Stanford University Press, 1966. Pp. 204–222.

Ellis, H.   *Studies in the psychology of sex.* Vol. 1. New York: Random House, 1936.

Erikson, E.   *Childhood and society.* New York: W. W. Norton, 1950.

Fauls, L. B., & Smith, W. D.   Sex role learning of five-year-olds. *Journal of Genetic Psychology*, 1956, **89,** 105–117.

Filler, W., & Drezner, N.   The results of surgical castration in women under forty. *American Journal of Obstetrics and Gynecology*, 1944, **47,** 122–124.

Ford, C. S., & Beach, F. A.   *Patterns of sexual behavior.* New York: Harper & Row, 1951.

Frank, L. K.   Cultural control and physiological autonomy. In C. Kluckhohn, H. A. Murray, & D. M. Schneider (Eds.), *Personality in nature and society.* New York: Alfred A. Knopf, 1953. Pp. 113–116.

Freedman, D. G.   Personality development in infancy: A biological approach. In S. L. Washburn & P. C. Jay (Eds.), *Perspectives on human evolution.* New York: Holt, Rinehart & Winston, 1968, Pp. 258–287.

Freud, Anna.   *The ego and mechanisms of defense.* New York: International Universities Press, 1946.

Freud, S.   The passing of the Oedipus-complex. In *Collected Papers.* Vol. II. London: Hogarth Press, 1924. Pp. 269–282.

Freud, S.   Some psychical consequences of the anatomical distinction between the sexes. In *The Standard Edition,* Vol. XIX. London: Hogarth Press, 1925. Pp. 248–258.

Freud, S.   *New introductory lectures in psychoanalysis.* New York: W. W. Norton, 1933.

Freud, S.   A child is being beaten: A contribution to the study of the origin of sexual perversions. In *Collected Papers,* Vol. II. Trans. under supervision of J. Riviere. London: Hogarth Press, 1948. Pp. 172–201. (a)

Freud, S.   Female sexuality. In *Collected Papers,* Vol. V. Trans. under supervision of J. Riviere. London: Hogarth Press, 1948. Pp. 252–272. (b)

Freud, S.   The psychogenesis of a case of homosexuality in a woman. In *Collected Papers,* Vol. II. Trans. under supervision of J. Riviere. London: Hogarth Press, 1948. Pp. 202–231. (c)

Freud, S.   Some psychological consequences of the anatomical distinction between the sexes. In *Collected Papers,* Vol. V. Trans. under supervision of J. Riviere. London: Hogarth Press, 1948. Pp. 186–197. (d)

Freud, S.   *An outline of psychoanalysis.* New York: W. W. Norton, 1949.

Garai, J. E., & Scheinfeld, A.   Sex differences in mental and behavioral traits. *Genetic Psychology Monographs*, 1968, **77,** 169–299.

Garn, S. M.   Fat, body size, and growth in the newborn. *Human Biology*, 1958, **30,** 265–280.

Garn, S. M., & Clark, L. C., Jr.   The sex difference in the basal metabolic rate. *Child Development*, 1953, **24,** 215–224.

Ginsburg, B. E.   Coaction of genetical and nongenetical factors influencing sexual behavior. In F. A. Beach (Ed.), *Sex and behavior.* New York: John Wiley & Sons, 1965. Pp. 53–75.

Gough, H. G.   Identifying psychological femininity. *Educational and Psychological Measurement*, 1952, **12,** 427–439.

Goy, R.   Unpublished paper presented at Conference on Sex Research, University of California, Berkeley, 1965.

Grunt, J. A., & Young, W. C.   Differential reactivity of individuals and the response of the male guinea pig to testosterone proprionate. *Endocrinology*, 1952, **51,** 237–248.

Hamburg, D. A., & Lunde, D. T.   Sex hormones in the development of sex differences in human behavior. In E. E. Maccoby (Ed.), *The development of sex differences*. Stanford, Calif.: Stanford University Press, 1966. Pp. 1–24.

Hampson, J. L.   Determinants of psychosexual orientation. In F. A. Beach (Ed.), *Sex and behavior*. New York: John Wiley & Sons, 1965. Pp. 108–132.

Hampson, J. L., & Hampson, J. G.   The ontogenesis of sexual behavior in man. In W. C. Young (Ed.), *Sex and internal secretions*. Vol. II. Baltimore: Williams & Wilkins, 1961. Pp. 1401–1432.

Hardy, K. R.   An appetitional theory of sexual motivation. *Psychological Review*, 1964, **71,** 1–18.

Harlow, H. F.   The heterosexual affectional system in monkeys. *American Psychologist*, 1962, **17,** 1–9.

Harlow, H. F.   Sexual behavior in the rhesus monkey. In F. A. Beach (Ed.), *Sex and behavior*. New York: John Wiley & Sons, 1965.

Harrington, C.   *Errors in sex role behavior*. New York: Teachers College Press, 1970.

Hartmann, H., & Kris, E.   The genetic approach in psychoanalysis. In *Psychoanalytic study of the child*. Vol. I. New York: International Universities Press, 1945.

Heilbrun, A. G., Jr.   An empirical test of the modeling theory of sex-role learning. *Child Development*, 1965, **36,** 789–799.

Helson, R.   Generality of sex differences in creative style. *Journal of Personality*, 1968, **36,** 33–48.

Jersild, A. T.   *Child psychology*. Englewood Cliffs, N.J.: Prentice-Hall, 1963.

Jones, E.   *The life and work of Sigmund Freud*. Vols. I & II. New York: Basic Books, 1953.

Jones, H. E.   *Development in adolescence*. New York: Appleton-Century-Crofts, 1943.

Jost, A.   Embryonic sexual differentiation (morphology, physiology, abnormalities). In H. W. Jones, Jr., & W. W. Scott (Eds.), *Hermaphroditism, genital anomalies and related endocrine disorders*. Baltimore: Williams & Wilkins, 1958.

Kagan, J.   The concept of identification. *Psychological Review*, 1958, **65,** 296–305.

Kallman, F. J.   Comparative twin study of the genetic aspects of male homosexuality. *Journal of Nervous and Mental Diseases,* 1952, **115,** 283–298. (a)

Kallman, F. J.   Twin and sibship study of overt male homosexuality. *American Journal of Human Genetics,* 1952, **4,** 136–146. (b)

Kallman, F. J.   Genetic aspects of sex determination and sexual maturation potentials in man. In G. Winokur (Ed.), *Determinants of human sexual behavior.* Springfield, Ill.: Charles C Thomas, 1963. Pp. 5–18.

Knop, C. A.   The dynamics of newly born babies. *Journal of Pediatrics,* 1946, **29,** 721–728.

Kohlberg, L.   Stage and sequence: The cognitive-developmental approach to socialization. In D. A. Goslin (Ed.), *Handbook of socialization theory and research.* Chicago: Rand McNally, 1969. Pp. 347–480.

Krafft-Ebing, R. *Psychopathia sexualis.* New York: Physicians and Surgeons Book Company, 1922.

Langer, J.   *Theories of development.* New York: Holt, Rinehart & Winston, 1969.

LeVine, R. A., & LeVine, B. B.   Nyansongo: A Gusii community in Kenya. In B. Whiting (Ed.), *Six cultures: Studies of child rearing.* New York: John Wiley & Sons, 1963.

Linton, R.   *The study of man.* New York: Appleton-Century-Crofts, 1936.

Linton, R.   *The cultural background of personality.* New York: Appleton-Century-Crofts, 1945.

Lipsitt, L. P., & Levy, N.   Pain threshold in the human neonate. *Child Development,* 1959, **30,** 547–554.

Lorenz, K.   Companionship in bird life. In C. H. Schiller (Ed.), *Instinctive behavior.* London: Methuen & Co., 1957.

Macfarlane, J. W.   Studies in child guidance: I. Methodology of data collection and organization. *Monographs of the Society for Research in Child Development,* 1938, **3,** (Whole No. 6).

Mason, W. A.   The social development of monkeys and apes. In I. DeVore (Ed.), *Primate behavior.* New York: Holt, Rinehart & Winston, 1965. Pp. 514–543.

Masters, W. H., & Johnson, V. E.   The sexual response cycles of the human male and female: Comparative anatomy and physiology. In F. A. Beach (Ed.), *Sex and behavior.* New York: John Wiley & Sons, 1965. Pp. 512–534.

Masters, W. H., & Johnson, V. E.   Human sexual inadequacy and some parameters of therapy. In M. Diamond (Ed.), *Perspectives in reproduction and sexual behavior.* Bloomington: Indiana University Press, 1968. Pp. 411–416.

Mead, M.   *Sex and temperament in three primitive societies.* New York: William Morrow, 1935.

Mead, M.   *Male and female.* New York: William Morrow, 1949.

Mead, M.   *New lives for old.* New York: William Morrow, 1956.

Mead, M.   Cultural determinants of sexual behavior. In W. C. Young (Ed.),

Sex and internal secretions. Vol. II. Baltimore: Williams & Wilkins, 1961. Pp. 1433–1480.

Mead, M.   *Culture and commitment: A study of the generation gap.* New York: Doubleday, 1969.

Metraux, R., & Mead, M.   *Themes in French culture.* Stanford, Calif.: Stanford University Press, 1954.

Millet, K.   *Sexual politics.* New York: Doubleday, 1970.

Mischel, W.   A social-learning view of sex differences. In E. E. Maccoby (Ed.), *The development of sex differences.* Stanford, Calif.: Stanford University Press, 1966. Pp. 56–81.

Money, J.   Components of eroticism in man: The hormones in relation to sexual morphology and sexual desire. *Journal of Nervous and Mental Diseases,* 1961, **132,** 239–248. (a)

Money, J.   Sex hormones and other variables in human eroticism. In W. C. Young (Ed.), *Sex and internal secretions.* Vol. II. Baltimore: Williams & Wilkins, 1961. Pp. 1383–1400. (b)

Money, J.   Chromosomal sex incongruent with gender role and identity. In *118th Annual Meeting, American Psychiatric Association,* Washington, D.C.: American Psychiatric Association, 1962. Pp. 38–39.

Money, J.   Developmental differentiation of femininity and masculinity compared. In *Man and civilization: The potential of woman.* New York: McGraw-Hill, 1963. Pp. 51–65.

Money, J., Hampson, J. L., & Hampson, J. G.   An examination of some basic sexual concepts: The evidence of human hermaphroditism. *Bulletin of the Johns Hopkins Hospital,* 1955, **97,** 301–319.

Moss, H. A.   Sex, age, and state as determinants of mother-infant interaction. *Merrill-Palmer Quarterly,* 1967, **13,** 19–36.

Moulton, R.   A survey and reevaluation of the concept of penis envy. *Contemporary Psychoanalysis,* 1970, **7,** 84–104.

Mowrer, O. H.   *Learning theory and behavior.* New York: John Wiley & Sons, 1960.

Murdock, G. P.   World ethnographic sample. *American Anthropologist,* 1957, **59,** 664–687.

Mussen, P. H.   Some antecedents and consequents of masculine sex-typing in adolescent boys. *Psychological Monographs,* 1961, **75** (2, Whole No. 506).

Mussen, P. H.   Long-term consequents of masculinity of interests in adolescence. *Journal of Consulting Psychology,* 1962, **26,** 435–440.

Mussen, P. H.   Early sex-role development. In D. A. Goslin (Ed.), *Handbook of socialization theory and research.* Chicago: Rand McNally, 1969. Pp. 707–731.

Mussen, P. H., & Distler, L.   Masculinity, identification, and father-son relationships. *Journal of Abnormal and Social Psychology,* 1959, **59,** 350–356.

Orlansky, H.   Infant care and personality. *Psychological Review,* 1949, **46,** 1–48.

Parsons, T.   Age and sex in the social structure of the United States. *American Sociological Review,* 1942, **7,** 604–616.

Parsons, T.   *Social structure and personality.* New York: The Free Press, 1964.

Parsons, T., & Bales, R. F.   *Family, socialization and interaction process.* Glencoe, Ill.: The Free Press, 1955.

Parsons, T., Bales, R. F., & Shils, E. A.   *Working papers in the theory of action.* New York: The Free Press, 1953.

Phoenix, C. H., Goy, R. W., Gerall, A. A., & Young, W. C.   Organizing action of prenatally administered testosterone proprionate on the tissues mediating mating behavior in the female guinea pig. *Endocrinology,* 1959, **65,** 369–382.

Rotter, J. B.   *Social learning and clinical psychology.* Englewood Cliffs, N.J.: Prentice-Hall, 1954.

Sanford, N.   The dynamics of identification. *Psychological Review,* 1955, **62,** 106–118.

San Francisco *Chronicle,* October 1968.

Schlegel, W. S.   Die konstitutionsbiologischen grundlagen der homosexualität. *Zeitschrift fur Menschliches Vererberung: Konstitutionslehre,* 1962, **36,** 341–364.

Scott, J. P.   Animal sexuality. In A. Ellis, & A. Arbarbanel (Eds.), *The encyclopedia of sexual behavior.* New York: Hawthorn Books, 1961.

Scott, J. P.   Review of *The naked ape: A zoologist's study of the human animal* by Desmond Morris. *Contemporary Psychology,* 1970, **15,** 374–375.

Sears, R. R.   Identification as a form of behavioral development. In D. B. Harris (Ed.), *The concept of development.* Minneapolis: University of Minnesota Press, 1957. Pp. 149–161.

Sears, R. R.   Development of gender role. In F. A. Beach (Ed.), *Sex and behavior.* New York: John Wiley & Sons, 1965. Pp. 133–163.

Skinner, B. F.   *Science and human behavior.* New York: Macmillan, 1953.

Skinner, B. F.   Critique of psychoanalytic concepts and theories. *The Scientific Monthly,* 1954, **79,** 300–305.

Sopchak, A. L., & Sutherland, A. M.   Psychological impact of cancer and its treatment. VII. Exogenous sex hormones and their relation to life-long adaptations in women with metastatic cancer of the breast. *Cancer,* 1960, **13,** 528–531.

Spiro, M. E.   *Kibbutz: Venture in utopia.* Cambridge, Mass.: Harvard University Press, 1956.

Stoller, R. J.   *Sex and gender.* New York: Science House, 1968.

Sullivan, H. S.   *Conceptions of modern psychiatry.* Washington, D.C.: William A. White Psychiatric Foundation, 1947.

Sutton-Smith, B., & Rosenberg, B. G.   *The sibling.* New York: Holt, Rinehart & Winston, 1970.

Sutton-Smith, B., Rosenberg, B. G., & Morgan, E. E.   The development of sex differences in play choices in preadolescence. *Child Development,* 1963, **34,** 119–126.

Tanner, J. M. *Growth at adolescence.* (2nd ed.) Oxford: Blackwell Scientific Publications, 1962.

Terman, L. M., & Miles, C. C. *Sex and personality.* New York: McGraw-Hill, 1936.

Tinbergen, N. Some recent studies of the evolution of sexual behavior. In F. A. Beach (Ed.), *Sex and behavior.* New York: John Wiley & Sons, 1965. Pp. 1–33.

Waxenberg, S. E. Some biological correlatives of sexual behavior. In G. Winokur (Ed.), *Determinants of human sexual behavior.* Springfield, Ill.: Charles C Thomas, 1963. Pp. 52–75.

Weller, G. M., & Bell, R. Q. Basal skin conductance and neonatal state. *Child Development,* 1965, **36,** 647–657.

Whalen, R. E. Sexual motivation. *Psychological Review,* 1966, **73,** 151–163.

Whiting, J. W. M., Kluckhohn, R., & Anthony, A. The function of male initiation ceremonies at puberty. In E. E. Maccoby, T. Newcomb, & E. Hartley (Eds.), *Readings in social psychology.* New York: Holt, Rinehart & Winston, 1958.

Wirz, P. *Die marind-anim von Hollandisch-Sud-New Guinea.* Hamburg: L. Friederichsen, 1922.

Young, W. C. The organization of sexual behavior by hormonal action during the prenatal and larval periods in vertebrates. In F. A. Beach (Ed.), *Sex and behavior.* New York: John Wiley & Sons, 1965. Pp. 89–107.

Young, W. C., Goy, R., & Phoenix, C. Hormones and sexual behavior. *Science,* 1964, **143,** 212–218.

Zelditch, M. Role differentiation in the nuclear family: A comparative study. In T. Parsons & R. F. Bales (Eds.), *Family, socialization and interaction process.* Glencoe, Ill.: The Free Press, 1955. Pp. 307–351.

AUTHOR INDEX

A

Aberle, D. F., 54
Anthony, A., 69
Aronson, L. R., 18

B

Bacon, M., 1, 74
Baker, H. J., 35
Baldwin, A. L., 49, 55, 56, 61
Bales, R. F., 57, 58, 59
Bandura, A., 49, 52, 83
Barr, M. L., 26
Barry, H., 1, 74
Bateson, G., 71
Beach, F. A., 14, 15, 16, 21, 22
Bell, R. Q., 26
Bertram, E. G., 26
Block, J., 65

Bremer, J., 28
Brim, O. J., 57, 63, 64
Bronfenbrenner, U., 52
Broverman, D. M., 25
Burns, R. K., 29

C

Carr, D. H., 26
Caspari, E. W., 13, 16
Chang, C. Y., 13, 18
Child, I. L., 1, 74
Clark, L. C., Jr., 26
Coffrell, L. S., 64
Costello, N. S., 26

D

D'Andrade, R. G., 74, 75
DeVore, I., 17, 18, 20, 21, 22

SUBJECT INDEX

Rosenberg, B

SEX AND IDEN

New York: H

113 pages